# DEATH
# TAXES
## AND OTHER
# ILLUSIONS

**Also by Arnold M. Patent:**
You Can Have It All

# DEATH
# TAXES
## AND OTHER
# ILLUSIONS

**ARNOLD M. PATENT**

**CELEBRATION PUBLISHING**
**PIERMONT, NEW YORK**

# ACKNOWLEDGEMENTS

I wish to thank the following people:

Selma Bokor for editing and tirelessly retyping the many drafts I submitted; David Garfinkel for his many insights, which broaden the book's audience; Katharine Deleot, Jim Bolen, Jed Diamond, and Dr. Joyce Abbott for their valuable suggestions; Steve, Donna, and Leonard Schwartz for their devotion to the printing and distribution of my books; the participants at my workshops, who provided me with the opportunity to expound my ideas and whose encouragement led to the writing of this book; the members of universal principle support groups for their dedication to integrating the principles into their lives; the coordinators of my workshops for their loving support of all participants; the performers at my workshops for sharing their special gifts; Grady Claire Porter for her unconditionally loving support; and Melva and Jesse Johnson for being perfect models of support for the entire support group network.

To my grandchildren, Vanessa, Evan, Benjamin, and Alison, who remind me that only love is real; to my children, Barbara, Paul, Sharon, and Morris, for their commitment to family; to my wife, Selma, for her unconditional love, nurturing presence, wit, and wisdom.

My purpose in writing this book is to express my ideas and feelings about illusion and principle clearly, simply, and lovingly. I hope to touch and inspire the reader so that together, we may feel our unconditional love and support for each other, just the way we are.

# CONTENTS

# PREFACE

From the time I was old enough to have a sense of what life was about, perhaps at age five or six, I lived life in a hurry. I was always trying to live tomorrow today. As a result, I did not allow myself to enjoy where I was or what I was experiencing. I continued to live this way for most of the first half-century of my life.

Then I came across some of the ideas that I later referred to as universal principles. I realized that they had been a part of me for a long time. They stayed inside largely because within the environment in which I lived and worked, I found so few people who cared to listen to what I had to say. They contradicted me because I used the adversarial approach I had learned during my legal career and this antagonism caused continual conflict within me. I finally gave up this approach and chose a forum that allowed me to express what I thought and felt.

More and more people became interested in my presentation and, to my surprise, I became a seminar leader. At one of my seminars, someone suggested that a book should be written about the material I was presenting. I agreed, and started to look for a suitable author. It took more than a year for me to realize that I was meant to be the author. Not having written anything more formal than compositions in high school and college, and legal documents during my career as a traditional lawyer, I was surprised at the ease with which the ideas I had expressed at seminars came together in a book.

The book, *You Can Have It All,* describes and defines the principles. It is not, however, a prerequisite for reading the present book, which describes how these principles always influence everyone's life.

Universal principles are a natural endowment. We do not have to learn them. We simply have to develop the willingness to stop resisting them. All of the principles that are referred to or described in this book are simple and easy to understand.

The major challenge for me in my transition from living life in the fast lane to becoming comfortable with and integrating universal principles was to learn to slow down.

You are welcome to share my thoughts and feelings about life in the slow lane. What I learned from the slowing down process is that there is an inverse relationship between hurrying and true accomplishment. As I slowed down, I became more peaceful and my presence became more powerful. That is one of the many gifts the Universe presents to each of us as we move in the direction of living our lives according to universal principles.

During the past several years of expressing and living according to these ideas, they have become ever more meaningful to me. I have also noticed that many of these ideas that were viewed as totally impractical only a few years ago are now seen by a growing number of people as the only practical way to achieve a peaceful and fulfilling life.

Bringing universal principles into the context of everyday experiences is my lifelong desire. This book is my gift to myself. I hope you will enjoy reading it as much as I enjoyed writing it.

# INTRODUCTION

This is a book about illusions. An illusion is something that we think is real but is not. Reality is viewing life according to universal principles. People have found that by following these principles, or general guidelines, they are inspired to be loving and supportive of themselves, of each other, and of their environment.

These guidelines are simple and easy to understand. They continually remind us of our Oneness. We do not really learn universal principles; rather, we unlearn beliefs that are inconsistent with them. As we release ourselves from these beliefs, the recognition of our natural state becomes clearer. The period from the time we start releasing these beliefs to the time we have completed the shift is referred to as the transitional period.*

Age is not a factor. Infants are as conversant with universal principles as are adults. In fact, most infants and young children express these principles naturally, because they have not yet adopted the contrary beliefs of society.

The greatest stumbling block to acceptance of universal principles is our unwillingness to honor our basic equality with one another. We have been taught to believe that our success and our security is dependent upon being better than others. We believe that the opportunity to make more money or have more status and power, no matter how little more, places us in an advantageous position. We believe that there is room for only a limited number of successful and secure people, and each of us is fighting for one of

---

*This term is defined in the glossary at the back of the book. All terms followed by an asterisk throughout the book will be found there, too.

those places. The fight is over a phony issue. The irony is that as we strive to achieve success and security, we invariably attain its opposite—a need for even more success and a nagging insecurity.

Principle tells us that not only are we all equal but it is also possible for each and every one of us to enjoy the fullness of life. In fact, the more we share, the more there is to share.

*You Can Have It All* defines and describes the principles. This book illustrates them through the common experiences we have with one another, topic by topic. It identifies and explains the principles involved in education, money, politics, support, equality, competition, relationships, and most of the other subjects we find ourselves dealing with in our daily lives.

I trust you will enjoy this approach.

---

Note: I have taken the liberty of alternating the use of male and female pronouns. Words synonymous with God are capitalized.

# DEATH
# TAXES
## AND OTHER
# ILLUSIONS

# DEATH

If we define death as the total cessation of breathing and brain function, then we are describing the death of the physical body. The body is a mass of vibrating energy. Our consciousness slowed the energy so that we could experience life in human form.

Our consciousness, which is not defined or limited by our body, has the capacity to raise or lower the vibrational levels of our body. We are all familiar with these vibrational changes in our energy. When we feel happy, we experience higher vibrations. When we feel sad or angry, we experience lower vibrations.

When the vibration slows down sufficiently, the result is what we term physical death. These changes in vibration do not affect the life force within the body, which does not stop or die.

There is an Intelligence greater than conscious-mind intelligence. The energy of this Intelligence supports all of life, which continues to expand infinitely. Having been created by this Intelligence, we can access It whenever we open ourselves to It. However, It speaks to us more softly than our conscious minds. Thus, we must allow the louder voice of the conscious mind to recede and become quiet as we listen to the still, small voice within.

This Intelligence is our intelligence, if we are willing to see ourselves in this way. Our consciousness, which derives from this Intelligence, has no inherent limit. It is only our limited beliefs that define us as the equivalent of our body.

The material in this book is not presented to prove anything. It is presented to bring gently to light society's assumptions, and to look at them from the viewpoint of principle. It is addressed only to those who find these ideas appealing or who are willing to set aside their preconceived beliefs for at least a little while. There is no intent to convert or argue with anyone.

It is in this spirit that I invite you to consider the thoughts presented here. Can they be proved scientifically? No, not by current scientific measures or instruments. But neither can scientists prove that all life begins at the moment of conception, or that all life ends at the moment of death.

We are left with a choice. The only practical solution is to select what works best for us. If we stop to consider, we will realize that there is nothing to lose and everything to gain when we open our minds to this way of thinking.

Let us assume for the moment that life does in fact continue after the death of the physical body. By believing this, we do not diminish the quality of our lives while on Earth. In fact, by releasing the fear* of death, we improve the quality of our lives quite considerably.

Fear is a major deterrent to a peaceful, joyful, and abundant life. A great deal has been written about so-called negative experiences that fearful people attract into their lives. Much has also been written of how the absence of fear leads to better performance at work, at home, and in all creative endeavors.

Many studies have also shown that fear reduces the survival probability in crisis situations. For example, a swimmer who finds himself carried out to sea by a wave is less likely to make it back to shore if he panics. Fear weakens and discourages a person. It impedes creative problem solving.

On the other hand, a person who believes that true death is impossible looks at life from a totally different perspective. He removes himself from day-to-day concerns more easily and takes a broader, more philosophical view of life. He is more peaceful and compassionate. Believing that there is no urgency in any particular situation, he adopts a more joyful attitude. The willingness to release one's belief in the finality of death is a freeing, self-empowering and self-loving step.

----

*An asterisk following a word or phrase indicates that a definition for this concept can be found in the glossary at the back of the book. The asterisk will be used only the first time the concept appears.

# AGING

There is a basic assumption in our society that the aging process is inevitable. Some people may age more gracefully or more slowly than others, but everyone ages. It is also assumed that aging means progressive physical deterioration of the body.

Those who attempt to forestall the process might use diet, exercise, cosmetic surgery, or vitamins to do so. Since such people believe that the process is physical, they attempt to deal with it by addressing only the body.

According to principle, our body as a mass of vibrating energy is dependent upon our consciousness for its state of being.

Consciousness is free to believe whatever it wishes. When our consciousness believes that life is a struggle, we bring about and experience struggle. On the other hand, if our consciousness believes in ease and simplicity, we create a life consistent with that belief. Since our consciousness may contain or adopt an infinite variety of beliefs, each of us experiences life differently—but always in accordance with the beliefs of our consciousness.

It is important to maintain clarity on the definition of consciousness. Since it is a part of the Soul, consciousness is eternal. None of us created our life Essence, our Soul, nor can we uncreate it. We do not die. However, we do determine, through free will, the quality of our lives.

Consciousness undistorted by belief systems is a reflection of its Creator. When we release choices and beliefs inconsistent with our true natures, we align with our Essence. This release process is a surrender of our conscious mind—with its self-created belief systems—to our intuition, our inner knowing.

9

The process of surrender does not mean loss of freedom. It means opening ourselves to our inner being, the source of our true creativity and free expression.

Consciousness in its undistorted form expresses unconditional love.* We were created in love to share and expand that love. Through our free will, we make choices to see life as we wish. However, when these choices are not loving, they become super-imposed on our true nature, which is a loving nature. We cannot change our essential being. It will forever remain a loving Essence, awaiting our total surrender to it.

As we continue the process of surrender, more and more of our true nature emerges. Expression of this loving part supports each of us and all others. Loving ourselves and others unconditionally raises our level of vibration and allows our physical being to remain vital.

# TAXES

There is a popular saying, "In this world nothing is certain but death and taxes." Death has been discussed in Chapter 1. As for taxes, consider the many people who pay no taxes: Poor people pay no taxes, and some wealthy retired people who have put all their assets in tax-free investments also pay no taxes.

The inaccuracy of the proverb is of some importance. What is more important is that it tells us that life is filled with distasteful circumstances—*and they are inevitable.* People who believe the saying—and many do—are living a life of little joy. They are plagued by a feeling of hopelessness and helplessness.

A fair question to ask such a person is "Why bother to go on living?"

The truth is that not only are problems, unhappiness, and other uncomfortable and troubling situations not inevitable, but, in fact, they are very much under our own control. Everything we experience is a reflection of the state of our consciousness.

Life can be a beautiful, joyful, peaceful, and abundant experience every minute. Most of us do not yet believe that, so we do not experience it. We have been brainwashed to believe that life must be a struggle—peppered, if not filled, with pain.* Considering something different is a tremendous challenge.

Each chapter in this book addresses ways in which we can support ourselves and each other in reaching the beauty, joy, peace, and abundance* of life. First, however, we must open our minds and our hearts. Next, we must examine carefully, and feel fully, the approach to life described by what we call universal principles.

Taxation represents a way of sharing resources for the benefit of all. Decisions about allocating these resources are made by elected officials.

Government, at its various levels, provides many services, including education, social services, and roads. It also provides the legislative, executive, and judicial services that establish guidelines for interaction among its citizens.

While any of us might disagree with a particular law or allocation of government funds, the overall system works for the common benefit. As voting citizens, we can change our approach, and we often do. We are also free to take an active role in the system, if we wish. Our resistance and what it represents creates an interesting phenomenon. Two ways we show our support* for the system are by actively participating in community service and by paying taxes. When we resist doing these things, we are, in effect, resisting supporting ourselves.

There is a universal principle that can shed light on this paradox. The principle states that *we can give only to ourselves.* When we look at this principle in materialistic terms only, it appears to be inaccurate. However, we are not only material beings. In fact, the quality of our lives is determined by how we feel. We are essentially feeling beings.

The one commodity that is in general currency and in unlimited supply is love. We can give all the love we wish, and it always feels wonderful. Thus, regardless of what else we give to another, whether it has material value or not, when we give love, we are giving ourselves a gift beyond measure.

The gift of love, which is giving at the level of principle, is always a gift to ourselves. There is another part of this gift to ourselves that is equally valuable. When we give love, we not only feel wonderful and joyful, we also feel peaceful.

There are many in our society who have chosen differently. They seek money and its counterparts, power and status. The inaccurate assumption made by these people is that such goals will bring them inner peace ultimately.

In our society, the race to make money and gain power and status generally involves competition, aggressive behavior, and a belief that there is not enough for everyone. The assumption that the attainment of money, power, and status will eventually lead to inner peace conflicts with another basic principle, which states that

12

*means and ends\* are identical. The means selected to achieve a particular end, in fact, generates the end.* If we choose competition to achieve a result, we are left with the energy of competitiveness, or separateness from others, as a result. Whenever we separate ourselves from others, for any reason, we feel a discomfort—the opposite of inner peace.

Other fallacies in the belief that chasing money will ultimately lead to a life of inner peace are the corollary beliefs that "nice guys finish last" or "no pain, no gain." This reasoning underestimates the value and power of inner peace.

Have you ever been in the company of a peaceful person? Most people enjoy being in the presence of this energy. The range of material wealth of these people varies greatly because wealth is not their primary consideration. They know that in order to experience inner peace, the quest for peace must be the primary motivating factor in their lives. At first look, this appears to be a risky choice. You ask, "If I focus on inner peace, where does the money to pay the rent and buy the food come from?"

# EARNING A LIVING

Where does the money come from to buy food, housing, clothing, and all the other things we require? The assumption is that everyone, or at least someone in each family, has to earn a living. The notion of earning a living is deeply imbedded in the consciousness of our society. In generations past, men took on this responsibility for their families. In the present generation, many women undertake this responsibility.

Earning a living is usually a full-time endeavor. The average person is tired when it is done or over. This often narrows the options that seem a[vailable]...

Principle states [that] abundance is the natural state of affairs in the Universe. If anyone is experiencing less than total abundance in each and every area, it means that the person is actively resisting or pushing away the abundance. This contributes greatly to our present and long-standing world problems. The acceptance of it requires more than most of us realize.

As a universal principle, abundance resonates with the core of our being. To actually feel and resonate with principle, we must be in a state of inner peace. When we are in such a state, our hearts are open. In other words, love and inner peace are constant companions. This is the setting in which principle is accessed.

Let us look at persons who have achieved inner peace. They shed light on the concept of abundance. One of the reasons there is such a variation in their wealth is that for those who live according to universal principles, wealth is unimportant. It flows in their lives to the extent required to appropriately serve their needs.

It is a fallacy that only large amounts of money contribute to a life of peace and joy. Many people live well on moderate incomes.

Abundance is a very broad and encompassing concept. The narrow focus on money invariably results in a lack of appreciation of the extraordinary abundance all around us. Is there any experience more abundant than being in the presence of someone who loves you very deeply?

The gift of life, one of the most generous gifts ever given, is the most perfect example of principle. All gifts given in the spirit of principle carry with them the love and joy of the giver and can only be enjoyed when the feelings, intentions, and generosity of the giver are honored.

Since life is a gift to each of us, no one can earn the right to life.

The gift of life includes our talents and unique qualities. We show appreciation for this gift by fully and freely sharing these talents and qualities.

Generosity begets generosity. When I give of myself fully and freely, I naturally encourage others to do the same. Generous people receive generously from others. Placing conditions and requirements around this perfect system only blocks the natural flow.

The belief in having to earn a living is a way we express resistance to abundance and all other universal principles. It is evidence of our belief in separation from our Source and from each other.

The creation of each of us in unconditional love remains the truth about all of life. It cannot be earned. It can only be enjoyed and appreciated. Gratitude is the way in which the gift is honored and allowed to expand.

Gratitude is appreciating what we have just the way it is. How many pages could we fill with lists of things that are gifts to us from the Universe and totally without cost? The warmth of the sun and the coolness of the rain, the joy of children and animals, the compassion of friends and family, the feeling of fulfillment from sharing our natural talents—these are just a few of the free gifts that are available to us.

Through our love for each other we enjoy providing the things each of us requires to live a comfortable life. Through our love for ourselves we allow others to give these gifts to us. This has nothing to do with working.

Remember, abundance is the natural state of affairs in the Universe. Each of us is a vehicle of this abundance. Some love to grow food, others love to cook it. Some love to plant trees, others love to cut them into boards, and still others love to build structures with the boards.

The motivation for the system is love. We have tried to convince ourselves that the motivation lies in having to earn a living or in the greed that pushes people to acquire more and more material things. We don't believe this in our hearts, and it is our hearts that control our lives when we allow our true nature to emerge.

At the beginning of this chapter I asked, "Where does the money come from to buy food, housing, clothing, and all the other things we require?" I noted the changes that are required in our consciousness for us to experience abundance, which includes all the material support we require. In later chapters I shall expand on these ideas and add to them. However, at this time I would like to answer the question in more concrete terms.

Outwardly, things look the same. Money continues to move from person to person, in most instances, as a result of payment for products or services delivered. From the standpoint of feeling, there is a major difference between a person who is working for a living and a person who has integrated principle. For the latter person, the product or service offered is an expression of what she loves to do. It is enjoyable and fulfilling and is not the result of work or effort.

Another difference is that the person who is aligned with principle enjoys being generous, just for the fun of it. Generosity begets generosity. It both eases the flow of money and expands it.

The abundance of the world is eagerly shared by everyone who opens to his true self. The abundance of the world is experienced through the concept of giving and receiving.* Our real selves know it is a joy to give as well as to receive. We also know in our hearts the principle of giving and receiving which is that *we can only give to ourselves.*

17

A true gift, which is giving at the level of principle, is always an experience of joy. It is the ultimate expression of self-love and opens us to receive more of the abundance of our abundant Universe.

# ECONOMICS

Economics is the study of ideas and factors that influence the production and distribution of goods and services. In our society, we have chosen a capitalistic system. The basic tenet of this system is that the reward of money is the most efficient way to stimulate the production and distribution of goods and services. Money is an effective vehicle to assist in this process, particularly when large numbers of people are involved.

A problem arises when many people perceive money as a desirable commodity in its own right and seek to collect it beyond its value as a medium of exchange. The time and energy expended by these people does not necessarily result in the production of goods or the creation of services that add to the joyfulness of anyone's life.

There are varieties of material goods, such as soaps, cereals, and perfumes that are redundant. The major motivation for their production, marketing, and distribution is the desire to accumulate dollars. This desire often reaches absurd proportions. An example is when a company purchases the patent to a superior product to stop its production, in order to protect the market for its existing product.

The desire to accumulate dollars sometimes creates a conflict of interest for doctors, lawyers, and other professionals. In order to increase their income, they may give advice or use procedures that needlessly complicate a situation. For example, there are reports from time to time of unnecessary surgery by physicians, or encouragement of exaggerated claims of injury by lawyers.

In our society, a strong motivation to create profits can come at the expense of the quality of the product. Residential builders often choose minimum standards of construction and inferior materials, giving little or no consideration to the maintenance problems created for the purchaser. The automobile industry has for many years taken a similar approach. Legislation is often required to protect the consumer from the results of the profit motive of manufacturers and purveyors of services.

Much has been written about the military-industrial complex in our country and the conflict of interest it generates. Peace is feared by many who believe their livelihoods or their wealth are dependent upon the continuation of the status quo. The desire for financial gain often leads to corruption in government.

The basic question that these distortions in our system raises is "Can we provide a comfortable standard of living for our citizens with a system that does not have the accumulation of money as its prime focus?"

Let us take a look at principle for the answer. It suggests that the first step is to define the purpose of the economic system. Let us choose the following: to support each other in a loving manner by offering products and services that are an expression of each of us doing what we love, leading to the peacefulness and joyfulness of all.

In support of this purpose, it is important to remember the definition of abundance. Since true abundance is achieved by opening ourselves to it, rather than by trying to bring it about, we require approaches that are in alignment with this principle.

Whenever a person or a society chooses the accumulation of money as a primary goal or purpose, peacefulness and joyfulness do not follow. It is also important to remember not to limit our definition of abundance to money alone.

Now let us examine an alternative economic system as a way of living our lives according to principle. We can do this within any larger society, regardless of its form. This system can be used by any individual or any group, no matter what its size. Participation is voluntary and does not create a conflict with any other system that coexists with it.

The system offered is the mutual support system, based on universal principles. It does not require anyone to do anything differently, it only requires the person to *perceive* things differently. Many people have followed a system of mutual support for several years, and most of the participants have achieved significant improvements in the quality of their lives.

Each of us is an expression of the abundance of the Universe. Joining together in loving support is a simple way of expanding that abundance. This is one of the principles on which the mutual support system is based.

An underlying assumption of the mutual support system is that we are all equal; that one person's skills or talents are not more valuable than another's—rather, all of them are equally valuable.

# EQUALITY

The concept of equality is in our basic political documents from equal rights to equal justice and equal opportunity. Though we acknowledge the concept in theory, in practice we promote the opposite. Statistics show that most of the wealth in our country is controlled by a very small percentage of the population. Since money equals power in our society, the rich are "more equal" than the poor in terms of access to material comforts, quality education, and mobility within the society.

The universal principle underlying equality is that *we are all One*. Another way of stating this is that in essential ways we are all the same. Each person feels the need to love, be loved, and live harmoniously in an environment of mutual support. Each individual is eager to share, knowing in her heart that abundance is the natural state of affairs in the Universe, and that when one of us is disadvantaged, all of us are.

The practice of inequality arises from the resistance to allowing our true selves to emerge. This resistance is an expression of fear. In principle, *fear is defined as a withholding of love—always from ourselves, and usually from another*. If love is everyone's inner need, how, then, does fear turn out to be the motivation for behavior in our society?

Life began when Infinite Intelligence created it. How we experience our lives is a result of how we view that Entity. Some of us perceive God as gentle and loving; others, as stern and wrathful. Still others see God as a protector. Whatever our personal belief, someplace deep inside almost everyone there is a sense of uncertainty and insecurity about God. Very few people feel in their hearts that God is loving and supportive under *all* circumstances.

One way we attempt to quiet this uneasiness is to seek preferred positions through education, experience, wealth, political power, or seniority.

The principle of equality reminds us that our fear of the Universe, and of each other, is not real. The willingness to perceive others as equals offers us the opportunity to feel the benefit of this change in perception. The Universe, as our Friend, will do the rest. It will demonstrate emphatically the benefits of this reperception.

All of the gifts of the Universe are available to everyone. Each of us has equal access to them. However, we block the experience of them as long as we perceive the need to create preferred positions for ourselves.

Equality tests our belief in the abundance of the Universe. When we truly believe there is more than enough for everyone, we shall share graciously and generously.

As we become more secure in our belief that we are equal, we allow our hearts to open to one another. It is through our hearts that we feel peaceful and joyful. It is also through our hearts that we feel the love and support of the Universe. This enables us to release our distrust of It. This sense of Oneness with each other and with the Universe creates experiences and circumstances that reflect our new view of life.

Most interesting is that those who achieve inner peace discover that the benefits of the material world are an unsought gift.

# MONEY

As we look at our society, it is hard to find a subject that dominates us more than money. National and international debts, cost of living, unemployment, taxes, and interest rates occupy much of our attention.

In our society, money functions as a medium of exchange. It has no inherent value but takes the value placed on it by its users. It is a way of facilitating the exchange of goods and services. Since money is a facilitator, the freer its movement, the more easily it accomplishes its purpose. In other words, the less restraint on its movement, the better.

A problem arises from money's secondary role—as a commodity in and of itself. We collect and accumulate dollars for their intrinsic value, just as we do the commodities that dollars are intended to facilitate. In fact, most of us perceive money as *the* most valuable commodity. However, when money is accumulated for other than loving purposes, its primary function as a medium of exchange is impeded.

Many economists are of the opinion that there are enough resources on our planet for everyone to live a comfortable life if the resources are shared in an equitable fashion.

If we accept the premise that the most important purpose of the members of a community is to lovingly support each other, then the more creatively we support this purpose, the more happiness we enjoy. The problem has always been—and remains—equitable distribution.

Working for money and accumulating it for other than loving purposes are clearly fallacies in our system. Often the main reason for its acquisition and accumulation is the fear that what it facilitates will not otherwise be provided. People are afraid that others will not voluntarily support them in maintaining a reasonable standard of living. Placing so much importance on money vests it with power.

Let us examine the validity of vesting money with power. Assume that a very wealthy person is driving in the country on the way to have lunch with a friend. Suddenly, his car stops and he cannot start it. He is many miles from the nearest house. He waits for another car to pass in hopes of receiving help, but no car appears. In this situation, money in and of itself has very little power.

With a little creativity, anyone can provide many examples of how powerless money really is. Its perceived power is just a function of our vesting it with power. The power in anything is a function of the power we attribute to it. We can vest paper clips with power if we choose to do so. In our society, we vest power in certain people, such as government officials, policemen, and members of organized crime. We can, with equal creativity, vest power wherever else we wish.

When power is vested externally, it weakens the person who sees power as being outside himself. In every situation, each of us chooses either to retain our power or give it away. We are encouraged to give it away, and we generally do.

How, then, do we reclaim it—or, better still, not part with it in the first instance? The answer lies in understanding the true source of power in the Universe. All power emanates from the Intelligence that created the Universe and everything in It. This Intelligence and power is in each of us, for we are of the same substance that created us and are thus endowed with all of Its attributes. Since It contains all knowledge, so do we. However, when we do not believe this, we behave as though it were not true. In fact, we assume the opposite is true, and then prove the accuracy of our belief by acting in accordance with it. Whatever our choice, we manifest results consistent with it.

Many of us are reclaiming our power by following the guidance of our inner knowing, our intuition. This requires releasing preconceived ideas and accepting all that flows to us. The more we open ourselves to receive without judgment,* the more we are given. One of the insights we gain in the process of relearning how to

Make decorating dreams come true with **Country Door**® *Credit!*

# COUNTRY DOOR® *Credit*

PRE-APPROVED CREDIT
OFFER EXCLUSIVE FOR

LINDSEY RUDDELL

DATE _____ 03-10-2023

one thousand and no/100 —————————— $1,000.00

MEMO **PRE-APPROVED CREDIT** _____ DOLLARS

Your **COUNTRY DOOR** Family

This Country Door® Credit certificate entitles you to a pre-approved line of credit for the amount shown.

[See terms of credit and pre-approved offer on the back of the order form.]

NON-NEGOTIABLE

This pre-approved credit certificate applies only to orders from Country Door Catalog Company, Monroe, Wisconsin. Cash value $00.00. OFFER EXPIRES 6/30/2023.

# COUNTRY DOOR®
*Credit*

- The decorator's account!

- Payments from $20 a month

- Makes ordering fast, safe & convenient

This pre-approved credit certificate applies only to Country Door Catalog Company orders, Monroe, Wisconsin. Cash value $00.00.

**OFFER EXPIRES 6/30/2023.**

**A. LOVE NEST BIRD HOUSE** Handcrafted out of solid wood with a distressed hand-painted finish. Hinged roof. Outdoor safe. 9½" w x 13½" h x 10" d.
NJ795116 ~~$29.99~~ NOW $24.79 Size/Wt. (A)‡

**B. WARM AND FUZZY SOCK GIFT SET**
Plush valentine socks inside a plastic heart ornament (4½" w x 4½" h). Polyester; machine wash. Imported. One size fits most.
NJ792810 ~~$11.99~~ NOW $4.79

receive is that abundance means much more than material wealth.

In our previous example of the wealthy person without assistance on a country road, abundance is a loving friend who notices that his guest is late, gets in his car and drives around trying to find him. Everyone is connected to everyone else, and when we are open, loving support arrives in what is often deemed a miraculous way.

Becoming comfortable with such a belief of connectedness requires a willingness to persevere during a transitional period, when old beliefs are not yet released and trust in universal principles is not yet total. In that sort of twilight zone, anything can happen, depending upon which belief is operative at the time. However, a person who is committed to mastery *does* succeed.

Signals of support are repeatedly given to encourage continuation of the commitment* to universal principles. At some point a shift occurs. This shift is from attachment to the material world, and the perception that money and other objects have power, to knowing that the Universe is a loving place of total abundance and whatever is required is available at the perfect time.

Each of us experiences money in the same way that we experience the rest of our lives. Money is a form of energy. All energy in the Universe is love. *The ease with which money flows in our lives relates to how loving we are to ourselves.*

Do not confuse a person who follows principle and experiences abundance with a person who makes money a primary goal and single-mindedly pursues it. There is no doubt that the focused pursuit of money, above all else, will produce a large amount of material wealth. However, the consequence of such an approach is clear. It is a feeling of discomfort that comes from superimposing an arbitrary system on the natural order of the Universe.

Making money a priority relegates other factors to less important positions. Thus, supporting associates and employees in a loving manner is usually overlooked. The time and attention devoted to family and friends is often less than is necessary to maintain a nurturing experience for all.

Seeking greater and greater profits often diminishes the product or service in some way. This deprives the provider of goods or services of the sense of fulfillment that comes from knowing and feeling that he has fully contributed to the joyfulness of the consumer's life.

Money is always a personal experience, even though it appears to be very impersonal. Like everything else, it reflects the state of our consciousness. Each person's present experience with money is an accurate description of his attitude toward it.

Money can be loved unconditionally and be a source of enjoyment for us, but first we must release all judgment about it. This is a major challenge, as we probably have more judgments about money than about any other subject.

Since money is only energy, an important rule in dealing with it is not to block its flow. If it is free to come and go, it flows comfortably in our lives. As much as is perfect stays, and the rest moves on. Reflecting the love and joy of its Source, money flows where love and joy are.

Attachment to money reflects a lack of trust in it and an unwillingness to share it generously. This results in less than ease and comfort in our relationship with it.

For the person who is at peace with it, trusts it, shares it generously, and loves it unconditionally, money flows abundantly, along with everything else.

Accumulating money, either out of a fear of being without it or to gain the perceived power and status that it brings, reflects a lack of unconditional love of it, and of self, and the experience with it is usually uncomfortable.

As a medium of exchange, money reflects our relationship with one another. For harmony in relationships, we trust each other as equals. This does not mean we must all have equal amounts of money. It means that those who have more or less than others do not see themselves, and are not seen by others, as more or less important.

True abundance is in infinite supply and flows easily in anyone's life who is willing to have an unconditionally loving relationship with it. This, of course, reflects an unconditionally loving attitude and approach to the Universe, to one's self, and to others.

As each of us allows more and more love to flow into our lives, our relationship to the material world becomes easier and simpler. We come to see the material world as a derivative experience in our lives. Making it the primary focus not only distorts our experience with the material world, it blocks the flow of love in our lives. This is the severest penalty we can inflict on ourselves.

To determine your relationship with money, ask yourself the following questions:

Do I love myself enough to allow money to flow easily and abundantly in my life?

Do I enjoy being generous to myself and to others?

Do I allow an abundant flow of money as a way of supporting myself and others in having more fun?

Am I aware that my value is not dependent upon having or not having money?

It is time to place money and the material world into proper perspective. They are wonderful mirrors for us. Are we willing to see only love, joy, and abundance reflected in them?

# SUPPORT

In our society, the giving and receiving of support begins with family and extends to friends. The primary motivation for this support is the love that members of the family and friends have for each other. This basic support is bolstered by institutions such as schools, social service agencies, and religious organizations.

The material support for families and the institutions that surround them is in the form of dollars—paychecks to individuals, taxes to government, and donations to charitable institutions. A relatively small amount of support comes from individuals who volunteer their services, although this support, though small, is very significant for all those who are touched by it.

In short, then, the motivation for earning dollars infuses society's support network. There is, however, a great price to pay for choosing a money-motivated, obligation-oriented support system instead of one that is voluntary and loving. Anyone who receives monetary support in place of loving support knows the difference and feels deprived.

*The Universe is a mutual support system.* It is designed as a vehicle to support the flow of unconditional love among Its components. Each of us craves participation, which is limited only by our resistance to honoring our basic natures.

It is abundantly clear that children raised in an environment where mutual support is a part of life grow up with an inner peace that leads them to value unconditional love and support more than anything else. As these individuals reach adulthood, they continue to live with these values. These are values we can all enjoy. All we have to do is make unconditional love and support our primary focus and money a secondary one.

This leads to the next question: Can people raised and trained in a competitive environment change their beliefs and patterns to function successfully in a mutually supportive environment? The answer is yes. In fact, many have joined one or more of a variety of existing support groups, some of which have been around for a long time. Included among these are self-help organizations, such as Alcoholics Anonymous and its many offshoots. This model of support has helped millions of people around the world to improve the quality of their lives. It is based on the voluntary offer of unconditional love and support.

One of the relatively recent support group networks uses a model based entirely on universal principles. (For a full description of how these support groups operate, and information on how to connect with the network of support groups, see the appendix.) People voluntarily come together to practice living their lives according to such principles. The format of the meeting is a series of exercises and activities, each of which is based on one or more of the universal principles. Experience with this model has shown that it is a simple and effective way of training people to live their entire lives according to universal principles. The goal of the group is, in essence, to learn how to live so that feeling unconditional love and support for each other becomes the primary motivating factor in their lives.

Inspired by a dramatic improvement in the quality of their lives, many participants have introduced the model to their families, businesses, and social organizations. Participants have discovered that unconditional love and support are indeed everyone's basic needs. When such love and support are freely and consistently given, the individuals are empowered to detach themselves from material things.

The sharing of unconditional love and support encourages each participant to feel love for herself. Since the amount of abundance we allow into our lives is directly related to how much we love ourselves, many participants open themselves to an increase in material comfort.

One of the greatest myths in our society is that people will be naturally lazy and unproductive if money ceases to play its present role as the primary reward for activity that society deems useful.

The mutual support group approach illustrates that the creativity released by sharing unconditional love and support is enormous. It inspires people to make products or offer services that they truly love and enjoy sharing with others. The quality of these products and services is much finer than of those that are produced by people motivated by a financial reward. Participants learn that money is really a nonissue in their lives. It is there, as is everything else, but as a support, rather than as a primary goal.

It is important to remember that universal principles, by their nature, are simple. Do not underestimate simplicity. It is the hallmark of genius. Infinite Intelligence, the guiding force in the Universe, operates at that level continuously.

The gifts of ease, simplicity, and abundance have been ours for the taking. Many people are now ready to accept these gifts and acknowledge their enormous value by sharing them lovingly and generously with others. They are amazing gifts. The more we give lovingly to each other, the more there is to give.

# INSURANCE

Insurance is a fascinating concept. Most people purchase many different kinds of insurance, such as life insurance, property insurance, medical insurance, and car insurance.

The assumptions behind the purchase of insurance are:

Life is full of uncertainties.

Some people are bound to suffer losses. Insurance then compensates for the loss through monetary reimbursement. It is an advanced social concept, allowing a large group to share risks that society believes are inevitable.

Principle tells us that there is no such thing as an accident. Each of us creates the events and circumstances of our lives. Life is a playing out of the state of our consciousness. If we believe in accidents, illnesses, economic challenges, and other such circumstances, we then see them occur in our experience.

Safety is a belief. Each of us experiences life precisely as we believe it to be. A person walks in fear in a neighborhood that is generally considered to be unsafe. She attracts an incident that justifies her fear. Others, feeling totally safe, walk in the same neighborhood without incident. The person who is fearful is judging the neighborhood or its inhabitants.

This leads to the definition of fear: the withholding of love from ourselves and often from another. The way to improve any situation that arouses fear is to be willing to feel love for all who are involved in the situation. However, in order to feel love, we must first release judgment.

What makes the world appear unsafe is merely the projection of our fear. We assume others are angry at us because we are withholding love from them. This derives from our underlying belief that God is angry at us because we are withholding love from Her.

For our lives to feel peaceful and safe, we must first make peace with our Creator. Often this is a long-term project. It is however, the only one that brings results that are lasting. Once we have trust in the Universe, everyone and everything becomes safe.

It is important to remember, however, that we are most self-supportive when we make decisions that are consistent with our actual beliefs. If a person is concerned about a medical emergency or a sudden loss of earnings, it is wise to honor the belief and act accordingly. It is not helpful to pretend we do not believe in something when we really do.

We can all change our beliefs. If we wish to modify them, it is best to complete the release of the old belief before acting in a way that is appropriate to the new one. For example, when I believe I shall no longer contract serious illnesses, it is appropriate to discontinue major medical insurance. On the other hand, if I am still uncertain as to whether I have released the belief in serious illness, it is wise to continue the insurance. Keeping insurance is not bad or wrong.

True trust in the Universe is a strong and complete knowingness. We act with confidence and peacefulness and move through life simply, easily, and joyfully. When there is doubt, it is intelligent to act in a way that takes doubt into consideration.

Is it really possible to withdraw all power from the physical world and feel it vested solely within? This is a question that each one of us answers for herself. The willingness to fully consider the question is a self-supportive way to proceed.

# AUTHORITY

What a powerful concept! Authority is one of the foundations for a rational society. We continually look for authorities to justify our decisions.

One of the basic rules of the legal profession is that an authority such as a law, or a court decision, by itself validates any conclusion adopted. A similar procedure is used in other professions. Historians use reports of earlier historical events to substantiate their interpretations of current events. Economists cite economic theories to forecast coming events.

So deep is our reliance on authority that we position authority figures such as policemen, judges, and government officials all around us. We also vest professionals such as teachers and doctors with authority. In business, authority is given to executives and managers. Labor, too, has its own hierarchy of authority.

From the viewpoint of principle, we have given our power away. In truth, however, there is no one outside of us who has any inherent power over us.

The eagerness to give away our power is a most interesting phenomenon in a society that is so attached to it. The paradox results from the misunderstanding of power and its true source. In transferring power to the symbols of authority in our society, we overlook the fact that we cannot give away what we do not already have.

The readiness to separate ourselves from our power points to a major unresolved conflict in our consciousness. Having failed to make peace with our Source, we cannot make peace with our own power.

We know in our hearts that the power in our Source and in ourselves is benign. We also know that reclaiming it means giving up our fear of our Creator, which is reflected in our fear of ourselves and of each other.

As we open ourselves to the power within, we question the symbols of authority outside ourselves.

Coming to peace with our power supports the realization that no one can truly harm us. We recognize that the power we vest in others is an illusion. We also recognize that a victim is someone who is unwilling to acknowledge who he really is. Through his lack of self-worth, he attracts people and circumstances that support his belief that life is unfair, people are uncaring, and calamity is inevitable.

There is an important step to take in reclaiming power: One must make peace with authority. Most of us have developed patterns of dislike and distrust of authority figures. This reflects our sense of separation from them. We can, when we are ready, open our hearts and love them just the way they are.

Each time any one of us reclaims her power, it encourages others to do the same. In the process, we ground the power in its true source, which is love. Love is the only power.

We can vest authority in another person and still remain her equal. We can also vest authority only in people who are caring, compassionate, and supportive.

The quality of our lives always depends on how much joy we allow ourselves to feel at any given moment. Joy is the feeling quality of love. Whenever we express love, we feel joy.

When we express more and more love, feel more and more joy, we become more and more powerful. It is a power that we enjoy sharing. As with all gifts in the Universe, there is no limit to them. They are an expression of the abundance of the Universe.

Whatever is real belongs to everyone equally and benefits all equally. We are our own power. We are our own authorities.

# PROBLEM SOLVING IN RELATIONSHIPS

Few people experience satisfying relationships most of the time. Psychologists, the professionals who study human behavior, cannot reach agreement as to the causes of, and treatment for, relationship problems.

Relatively few psychologists look to universal principles for the solution. Yet the way a lasting solution to a problem is found is by viewing it from the perspective of principle.

Let us look at an example of how principle can assist in solving a parent-child relationship problem. Consider a parent who is encouraging her child to eat. The parent's perception is that the child must eat to be healthy. The child, not feeling hungry, sees the parent as annoying and unreasonable. If a resolution is attempted using a traditional approach, no mutually satisfactory solution will be found. After unsuccessfully trying to induce the child to eat, the parent may threaten punishment. She perceives that her greater size and position of power can resolve the confrontation.

The child will probably respond by becoming more resistant. He sees the power play as being even more intolerable than the request to eat when he is not hungry. The parent sees the power play as being justified in order to maintain the child's health. However well intentioned, it does not persuade the child.

Now let's look at the situation from a different perspective. Universal principles are the highest standards by which to view anything and are a guaranteed solution to the problem. This does not mean that the person viewing the problem from the perspective of universal principles is ready to use the principles at that moment. It just means that the resolution is available whenever the person is ready to follow this guidance.

Principle tells us that both the parent and the child have an inner need to love each other. In the above example, each one's outer expression is both a demand upon the other for proof of unconditional love, and a withholding of love. The belief that eating a particular food at a given time will contribute to good health is just as much an illusion as the belief that resisting a parent's demands will cause a parent to stop making demands.

When the parent is ready to demonstrate unconditional love for her child, she will gain the child's cooperation in eating. Foods will be selected and schedules arranged that will be comfortable for both. This will be a natural outgrowth of expressing unconditional love for the child.

Many parents, not having received unconditional love in their own childhood, lack the understanding of how to express it to their children. Learning how to do this requires great commitment and intention. Joining a support group where unconditional love and support is the mode of behavior is very helpful. Such an environment encourages a willingness to forgive the child, and oneself, for past behavior.

The change in energy within the parent to a feeling of forgiveness, no matter how slight, is instantly communicated to the child. Energy travels rapidly throughout the Universe.

When any person in a relationship changes her perception of that relationship, the relationship changes. In this example, every time the mother feels a little more forgiveness for herself and her son, the son feels more love and acceptance for his mother.

In some cases, forgiveness by one person, while leading to a more loving relationship, allows the parties to recognize that they have vastly different life-style preferences. In the case of two adults, this can result in their spending less time with each other, or even parting. However, the basic relationship remains peaceful and loving.

In the case of parent and child, personality differences can be recognized and should be honored. Because of the greater awareness of the parent, it is her responsibility to balance her own preferences with those of the child. For example, the mother may be a quiet and reserved person who keeps her thoughts and feelings to herself. The child may be outgoing, talkative, and eager to share his experiences. The mother can allow the child time to share his experiences. The child, in turn, can allow his mother some quiet time. With the growth of the child, more or less time may be spent in the physical presence of the parent. However, love for each other continues to be the basis of the relationship.

It is important to continue with the forgiveness process until completion, even though the subject of the forgiveness is someone whose behavior or attitude makes it difficult for us to continue. Remember, when another person stimulates discomfort in us, she reflects the part of us that we have rejected.

Completion occurs when just thinking of the other person brings feelings of deep unconditional love. Unconditional love is indivisible. It is always to our advantage to feel more love in any relationship. This not only expands the love we feel in other relationships, it expands the love we feel for ourselves.

# MODELS

Society teaches us about life and relationships through the use of models. When we join together, we create models for the relationships. We have models in families, education, sports, business, and government, to name a few. The uncertainty, insecurity, and chaos that surround us reflect the less than perfect models we are using.

We know that we are ready to improve the quality of our lives when we create more perfect models, ones that are truly supportive, nurturing, and loving. We can create perfect models for all of our relationships once we have mastered a basic model of unconditional love and support.

A support group based on universal principles is such a model. After we are comfortable relating to one another using this format, it becomes the natural way we relate to everyone. Mastery of this simple structure is one of the greatest gifts we can give ourselves. It provides continual support for expressing love for ourselves and each other.

One of the most valuable features of such a support group is the opportunity it gives to each participant to ask for support in terms of universal principles. We have all been trained to ask for support from sources outside ourselves. We borrow money from each other and from banks to meet obligations. We complain to one another and look for sympathy when we feel rejected and unfairly treated.

What we haven't learned to do is ask for the kind of support that truly resolves the situation. Seeing the troubling situation in terms of principle gives us the key to the solution, though we might not yet be willing to give up our preconceived ideas to achieve the solution.

Some examples of the ways a request for support in consciousness can be made are:

## SHORTAGE OF MONEY

I ask for support in consciousness to feel the abundance of the Universe.

I ask for support in consciousness to feel gratitude for all that I presently have.

I ask for support in consciousness to feel that the Universe is on my side and is eager to share Its abundance with me when I am willing to receive it.

I ask for support in consciousness to recognize that I am blocking the flow of abundance into my life.

I ask for support in consciousness to be aware of the ways I block the flow of abundance so that I can avoid sharing it with others.

## RELATIONSHIPS

I ask for support in consciousness to open myself to the love and support of others.

I ask for support in consciousness to feel whole and complete by myself and not to seek a partner from a sense of need.

I ask for support in consciousness to become aware of my true power and beauty.

I ask for support in consciousness to feel lovable.

I ask for support in consciousness to feel my sense of equality with others.

I ask for support in consciousness to recognize that what I perceive as a rejection from others is really mirroring my rejection of myself.

I ask for support in consciousness to become aware of how much others are eager to love me.

## CAREER

I ask for support in consciousness to be in touch with my natural talent.

I ask for support in consciousness to allow myself to fully and freely express my natural talent.

I ask for support in consciousness to allow myself to receive support from others in sharing my talent.

I ask for support in consciousness to feel the connection between my talent and the abundance of the Universe.

I ask for support in consciousness to allow myself to experience the joy of expressing and sharing my talent.

I ask for support in consciousness to allow the abundance of the Universe to flow to me as I share my talent generously with others.

I ask for support in consciousness to experience the joy of giving and receiving* through the expression of my talent.

## FAMILY

One of the most effective uses of the request for support in consciousness is within the family. Giving each family member the opportunity to request support, while he is feeling the love,

45

support, and acknowledgment of the other family members, goes a long way toward creating family harmony. Each family member quickly learns that when any one of them feels supported, he is more willing to support the others. This simple procedure changes the family's dynamics from a few people living under one roof and making the best of a difficult situation to a team that is pulling together.

There is no limit to the mutually supportive models we can create. It is time to take advantage of this marvelous vehicle to improve the quality of our lives in a way that benefits everyone.

# SELF-RELIANCE, INDEPENDENCE, AND RUGGED INDIVIDUALISM

A basic ethic of our society is that we must prove ourselves by being independent and self-reliant. This is a particularly strong ethic among men, and it is growing rapidly among women.

A corollary ethic is that of competition, often causing behavior that is questionable by moral and ethical standards. Athletes take special drugs to improve their performances. Business people use elaborate schemes to control markets. Financial experts, lawyers, and accountants sometimes find legal ways to structure investments that violate the intent or spirit of a tax law or regulation. Religious leaders favor congregants who give large contributions.

Principle tells us that *the Universe is a mutual support system.* Every part is designed to be in support of every other part, and all parts are assumed to be of equal value. The sun and the rain work together to support life in plants and animals. One is not more important than the other. The musicians and the conductor in an orchestra are equally essential and of equal importance in creating a successful concert.

*A system of polarities, in which the individuals emphasize their differences and separateness instead of their Oneness, creates chaos and discomfort while harmony is patiently waiting to burst forth.*

47

The Universe, as a mutual support system, is always functioning perfectly, even though we don't always see It that way. How we view the system determines how we experience it. Seeing it as a haphazard, accidental, or chance system causes us to experience discouragement and, often, despair. Seeing it as an accurate reflection of the state of our consciousness, both individual and group, enables us to take the steps that will change our perceptions. One of the most efficient ways of changing our perceptions is through participation in a mutual support group.

How does a model of mutual support operate within a society of differing belief systems?

Mutual support is a system or model of choice. No one is compelled to use it. In fact, a basic assumption of a mutual support group is that participation is voluntary. It proves its value by demonstration. People who experience the model decide whether or not it is beneficial. Its value is determined by the quality of the model used (how closely it aligns with principle) and the degree of commitment the participants have to the model and to each other.

A mutual support group provides an opportunity for people to learn how to rise above their perception of differences and notice the ways they are alike. With the guidance of universal principles, they experience the joy and fulfillment of giving and receiving unconditional love and support. Participants also learn to accept each other and themselves just the way they are.

Some people ask, "How can a system where everyone is cooperating be any fun?" This question grows out of a lack of understanding of a mutual support system. It assumes that experience with the adversarial and competitive model provides a basis from which to assess the mutual support model. But that is not the case. For instance, skill in raising one's income and status as a corporate executive is not suitable preparation for raising one's perspective to see life in terms of universal principles.

What is helpful is the willingness to recognize the main assumption of a support group—*it is natural and enjoyable for people to give and receive unconditional love and support.*

Many people have at one time or another joined a group that attempted to function in a spirit of cooperation. If the result was less than supportive, the experience could have been misleading. When people who live in a competitive and adversarial society join a group that uses a model of cooperation, at first the result is often proof of the difficulty of switching models. Remember, a support group model requires completely different assumptions and agreements than does an adversarial and competitive one. Until a participant integrates the new assumptions, and is comfortable with them, his existing beliefs may cause him to conclude that a mutually supportive model is utopian and of no practical value.

Some of the other assumptions of a support group are:

Each participant, no matter what his background, age, credentials, or experience, is equal to every other participant.

Supporting another person means accepting him just the way he is.

How we view or perceive each other determines how we experience each other.

Changes in perception occur only when a person is ready. Readiness is encouraged by helping the person to feel loved just the way he is.

Why, then, is the model of mutual support so little known? The media seem to have overlooked the depth and breadth of the movement toward mutual support and cooperation. Concerts to provide financial support for poor and ill people, and the generous outpouring of worldwide support for people suffering from famine in Ethiopia, are deemed by many of us as transitory events, rather than evidence of a deep commitment to change. Yet millions of people in the United States alone buy books and tapes and attend seminars that teach and demonstrate the practice of such concepts as universal principles.

Though the percentage of the population with this commitment may be relatively small, the numbers are large. One percent of our population is 2.5 million people. More than that number of people are deeply involved in, and committed to, living their lives according to a form of universal principles, as best they can.

49

Everything in the Universe is purposeful, including the Infinite Intelligence that created it all. While it is beyond the rational mind to comprehend or describe what this purpose* contains in any complete way, aspects of it do emerge. A part of this purpose is to support each of us in recognizing and becoming aware of how our individual purpose relates to the purpose of the Universe.

One of the ways the Universe encourages us to move into alignment with universal principles is to give signals of support every time we do. Remember that free will is always honored by the Universe. The choice is ours, and that choice can lead to any decision at any time, including a sudden change of mind.

Every time a choice is made to align with the Universe, we feel Its support. The signal is clearly given. In the same way, a choice to move out of alignment causes signals of discomfort. This is the Universe's way of encouraging us to look at the situation differently and choose again.

Aligning with universal principles brings the core aspects of our being into awareness. Even when the outer behavior of a person who is in the process of aligning with the Universe appears no different from a person who remains guided by traditional beliefs, there is a vast difference.

For a person aware of principle, acting out of anger or fear is a signal to look at the situation differently. Such a person, when expressing anger, recognizes that someone else's behavior is not the cause of the anger.

Principle tells us that there is no such thing as good and bad. All discomfort is a result of seeing a person or situation inaccurately. Let us look at an example where the situation appears one way but is actually something else.

A man is seen dragging someone who is bleeding profusely while yelling at his apparent victim. For someone entering the scene in the middle, there is a temptation to intervene to prevent any further harm from coming to the bleeding man. The observer doesn't know, however, that the injured man was severely beaten by someone who left the scene but threatened to return shortly. The man who is yelling is trying to keep the victim from losing consciousness while he is being dragged to safety. The person doing the yelling is acting out of love and support. The person who came in after all this started can easily misunderstand what is happening.

We always enter a scene in the middle, and assume that since we perceive people acting in a certain way, their motives are consistent with our perceptions.

All life began in peace, harmony, abundance, and love. Using our free will, we embarked upon a mission to test and experience all of the other ways we can relate to each other.

Essentially, we are only capable of giving and receiving unconditional love and support. It is our basic nature. We had to learn how to be competitive, aggressive, and adversarial. To experience this, we created a scenario based on separateness, difference, and a withholding of love.

Globally, we have pushed our imaginations to the extreme. We have created ultimate weapons of physical destruction, debasing forms of political tyranny, seemingly unsolvable environmental pollution, gross economic imbalances, and hateful characterizations of countries with different ideologies.

We have tested the many ways we can live with one another without honoring our basic need to be loving and supportive. We have repressed this need for love and support, avoided it, distorted it, and manipulated it. It is now time to return to it, acknowledge it, surrender to it, and enjoy it. We are exhausted by our attempts to run away from it any longer. We are literally calling to each other in the only ways we know, beseeching one another to return to our basic natures.

Principle tells us that every unloving act is a call for love and support. This is particularly true of acts that appear to be angry and attacking. It is the key to our return to a life of peace and harmony. We must recognize that apparent anger and aggressiveness is grounded in frustration—based on a long period of forgetting who we are and what we truly wish from one another.

It is time for us to hear one another's call and to respond. All we need to do is to respond in love, and the caller will acknowledge in appreciation.

51

Either party in a relationship has the power to change the relationship. As soon as one person aligns with principle, the relationship changes. The choice to align with the Universe brings the power of the Universe to us, and we feel that power. It remains available to all who use it to expand the experience of love throughout the Universe.

There is no limit to the ways we can support each other. A relationship based upon principle is one in which we align ourselves with the Universe and, in partnership with It, explore the many ways we can express our love and support for each other.

# SELFISHNESS

The belief that each of us is responsible for his own success, coupled with the belief that the resources available are insufficient to allow everyone to be successful, leads many people to act in ways that are selfish.

Each of us defines success differently. For one person it may be finding a job that pays the rent and other basic expenses. For another it may be heading a major corporation. For yet another it may be helping third-world villagers to become self-sufficient.

When the goal is making more money or gaining more power, the means used to achieve the goal are invariably selfish. A worthwhile goal does not justify using other than worthwhile means to attain it. Principle tells us that *means and ends are equivalent. The means we use are, in fact, the end we achieve.*

What is the difference between being self-supportive and being selfish? Principle gives us the answer. It is contained in the concept of giving and receiving and in the principle underlying it, that *we can only give to ourselves.*

Something that is not generally understood is that *feelings are a basic cause in the Universe.* Giving in a spirit of generosity places the giver in a perfect position. Since we experience life as a mirror-image reflection of the state of our consciousness, being in a joyful state helps us to create experiences that are joyful.

Whenever we give and receive love, we create events and circumstances that mirror the joy that we feel within.

Why don't we do this more often if it is so simple? Each of us has been trained to withhold love. Boys are taught that it is a sign of weakness to be outwardly loving. Girls are taught that boys may take advantage of their loving feelings. Professionals are taught that it is unprofessional to allow feelings to intrude into a

53

relationship based on logic and objective analysis. Most of us are taught to be impartial. To ensure impartiality, we are cautioned to keep our feelings out of any decision making.

Feeling and expressing love is often perceived as dangerous. We are taught to trust our heads but not our hearts. Yet *love, being the only energy in the Universe, is always seeking expression.* When we repress it—that is, when we withhold feeling love for ourselves and others—we generate discomfort.

We cannot contain love. As energy, it must circulate. After passing through our belief systems, it can appear as anger, frustration, or another emotion.* However, the perception that the emotion is not love does not change the truth that only love is real. The simplest way to reach that reality is first to *feel the emotion fully, then accept it just the way it is,* and finally *embrace it lovingly.*

Since feelings are a causative element, denying ourselves the free expression of our feelings substantially limits the experience of love in our lives. The mirror principle* always applies. *When we feel loving, we generate loving experiences and loving people in our lives. When we withhold love, we attract unloving experiences and unloving people.* It is really that simple.

We have such a strongly vested interest in withholding love that it is very challenging to the average person to release it. The rules and practices of our society in training us to withhold love are not based solely on prior generations' practices. They are rooted in our withholding love from our Creator. This is why our resistance to change runs so deeply. It is also why strong intention and commitment, buttressed by regular support, is a prerequisite to expressing love in any consistent and trusting way.

We remain selfish in our relationships with others when we deny ourselves unconditional love and support. We express generosity in our relationships when we recognize that there is an infinite supply of it and allow ourselves to freely receive. In fact, the more unconditional love and support we give and share, the more we receive.

A related concept is self-esteem. The principle behind this concept is that *others will not support us more than we support ourselves.* If we place a low value on ourselves, others will do the same. This is unrelated to our true value.

How does self-esteem affect our experiences in the world? Let us look at a person with artistic talent. In order to discourage her from pursuing fine arts as a career, which they believe would not allow her to support herself, her parents tell her that she will never succeed as an artist. This discouragement causes her to doubt herself beyond her ability as an artist. Her need to express herself as an artist is so strong, however, that she becomes a professional artist anyway. Her self-doubts cause her to greatly undervalue her talent. Thus, she is unable to attract people who are willing to pay her what her paintings are worth.

It is only through consistently feeling unconditional love and support for being who we are, just the way we are, that enables us to build the sense of self that allows others to support us. It is also the only way we come to recognize that selfishness is really self-denial.

# PRINCE CHARMING AND THE BEAUTY QUEEN

The fashion and cosmetic industries, supported by advertising, television, and the movies, encourage all of us to place major importance on how we outwardly present ourselves. The way we appear is considered more important than who we are.

Yet the body has no life of its own. All life in the body comes from the life force within it. This life force has a consciousness that is free to believe whatever it wishes.

Since consciousness may contain or adopt an infinite variety of beliefs, each individual experiences life differently—but always in accordance with his beliefs.

It is important to remain clear about the definition of consciousness. As a part of the Soul, consciousness is eternal. We have already discussed the fact that none of us created our life Essence, our Soul, nor can we uncreate it. So we do not die. We do, however, through free will, determine the quality of our lives.

Consciousness is a reflection of its Creator. When choices and beliefs inconsistent with our true nature are released, we enjoy being supportive of one another. The process is a surrender of the conscious mind—with its self-created belief systems—to our intuition, our inner knowing.

The surrender process does not mean loss of freedom. It means opening ourselves to our inner being, the source of our true creativity and free expression. We were created in love to share and expand that love. Through our free will, we made choices to see

57

life differently. However, these choices, these beliefs, are superimposed on our true nature. We cannot change our essential being. It will forever remain a loving Essence, awaiting our total surrender to It.

As we continue the surrender process, more and more of our true nature emerges. Expression from this loving part supports us and all others.

Principle tells us that *successful relationships are based on the willingness of people to love each other unconditionally, just the way they are.* Advertising and the media bombard us relentlessly with the message that only by using the product offered or projecting a particular image we will have successful lives or relationships and we will be loved. Since our experiences mirror our beliefs, we know how deeply imbedded are our beliefs in the superficial aspects of life and relationships. With the divorce rate as high as it is, it is apparent that most couples who enter into marriage believe that the superficial aspects of each of them are real and important.

The difficulty we have in loving ourselves and each other just the way we are has led us to search for alternate ways of satisfying this basic need. The real reason for the difficulty is our failure to deal with the underlying issue—our ambivalent feelings about God.

We shall continue to focus on goals that undermine our peacefulness, our sense of safety in the Universe, and our joyfulness until we go back to basics. Having been created by an unconditionally loving God, we are all truly lovable just the way we are. It is time to acknowledge this and express it to ourselves and to each other.

# EDUCATION
# AND CHILDREN

Formal education is one of the cornerstones of our society. We use it primarily to indoctrinate children with society's basic beliefs. We assume that this will help the child become a successful adult participant in the community.

Most of what is taught is rote learning. Relatively little is done to support a child's creativity. Very little is offered to build a strong sense of self in each child. Children are not encouraged to be equals in the learning process. Rather, they are encouraged to feel dependent upon authorities—the people who insist that they know what is best. As a result, a very small percentage of students express creativity and free thinking in school, subsequently in their careers, and in their approach to life.

Considering the fact that we have so many teachers' colleges in our country, it is surprising to see how little has changed in the basic approach to education. This contrasts with the many changes that have occurred in our society and that require a parallel adjustment in our educational institutions.

Education is the way we maintain continuity in our society. In fairness to the educators, they are limited in their choices by the beliefs of the local communities that they serve.

Let us look at some universal principles in order to shed light on the educational challenges facing society. Principle tells us that *each individual, including each child, has access to Infinite Intelligence.* The assumption that children are born helpless and have to learn everything from the beginning is not accurate. Another mistaken assumption is that children must learn, and parents and teachers must teach. The truth is that *children and adults learn from each other.*

Each infant is born with talents and experiences that he has brought with him, and it is to everyone's advantage to acknowledge and encourage the full and free expression of each person's talent.

We presently have a distorted approach to talent. With society's offer of very large financial rewards for careers in business, finance, and some of the professions, we encourage many young people to choose these careers and to abandon talents that do not usually generate such large rewards. Thus, there is a shortage of teachers, mechanics, and carpenters, and an oversupply of lawyers and stockbrokers.

Under the principle of free will, we make choices as individuals and as a society. Though the choices are unlimited, each choice has a consequence. The consequence is not subject to choice. It is mandated. It is essential to understand this.

While everyone is free to choose how he wishes to act and think, that does not leave us free to choose the consequences of our actions and thoughts. For example, if I choose to withhold love from someone, I cannot also feel joyful. If I choose to make material wealth my primary objective, I cannot also feel inner peace.

Consequences are the way the Universe guides us toward mastery of universal principles. Time is not a factor at the universal level. Each person can take as long as he wishes to achieve mastery.

A way to simplify the process is to recognize the value of children. Children are accurate mirrors of the state of consciousness of their parents. Thus, parents can, if they wish, learn a great deal about themselves in a relatively short period of time.

In order to carefully listen to and learn from our children, we must truly respect and honor them. This is not only very supportive to them, but it also builds their sense of self. Current studies show that one of the greatest causes of children's problems is their inadequate sense of self.

The practical problem that we are dealing with is asking adults with relatively weak self-images to support children in a way that encourages a strong sense of self. The solution is simple. The adults must rebuild their own sense of self first.

When children are fully respected and honored, not only for their role, but also for their being just the way they are, we arrive at a balance point. It is the principle of equality, the recognition that everyone is truly equal to everyone else. Parents are not more important than children. Children are not more important than parents. Presidents are not more important than street cleaners. Street cleaners are not more important than dishwashers.

When we no longer need to rate and judge the various positions in our society, we shall be able to recognize that each child comes into this life with something of value that is crying out for recognition and support. It is only by honoring the uniqueness and value of each individual that society reaches its fulfillment.

This brings us back to the principle that *each person is entitled to be unconditionally loved and supported, just the way he is.* Out of this flows the encouragement for each individual to fully and freely express who he really is.

It is important to keep in mind that everything in the Universe is purposeful. Each of us reflects what we see in the other. It is only by honoring another—that is, loving him just the way he is—that we support him in bringing his purpose and his talent into alignment. This in turn benefits all of us.

Once we honor the role of the child, acknowledge him as an equal, appreciate that his life is purposeful and that he has a talent that is a gift of the Universe, we are ready to address curriculum.

The initial objective of a curriculum is to make learning a loving and joyful experience. When material is presented in an inspiring way by a teacher who loves what he is doing, children learn in a natural and joyous way. The talent of each child is supported and the various talents are brought together to broaden the experience of all.

Once that is attained, subject matter will be meaningfully and creatively integrated and utilized by the students.

As for the selection of teachers, there are only three prerequisites:

a sense of self that is loving and supportive;

a desire to unconditionally love and support children; and

a belief that teaching is an expression of a talent and is something the teacher loves to do.

We previously looked at the definition of abundance—the natural state of affairs in the Universe. A major part of that abundance is the role we play in each other's lives. As we genuinely nurture and support each other to become all we inherently are, we notice that we are surrounded by limitless abundance.

Just imagine a world in which everyone is doing only what he loves and enjoys, for the pure joy of it. The range of talents is so great that the products and services offered are of the highest quality. Everyone knows and feels the deep satisfaction that comes from supporting others.

This leads to the concept of models. The highest-quality model we can create is one based on universal principles. As we establish this model in our society, and learn to master it, we greatly simplify our lives. The more loving the model, the more supportive the experience that grows out of following the model.

The quality of our lives, which is how we feel at any moment, is always related to how open our hearts are. *The only way we can improve how we feel is by allowing ourselves to feel more love.* Each time any individual succeeds in improving the quality of his life, others learn that it is possible. This is what education is all about—each of us demonstrating the joy of improving the quality of life to each other.

Anyone is free to demonstrate a more loving and supportive model at any time. There is truly no limit to the creativity we can express or the joy we can share.

# TESTS AND LABELS

Access to schools and employment, and advancement thereafter, are often determined by scores on tests. Evaluation starts early in most people's lives, and parents usually determine the outcome. Even without the use of formal tests, parents decide how smart, talented, and desirable their children are. Most children accept these evaluations and are prepared to have other authority figures perceive them in the same way.

When formal testing begins, scores often reflect the child's existing beliefs about herself and further reinforce them. Having been labeled, the child usually devotes the rest of her life to validating the label.

Labeling works very well. However, most people fail to utilize its positive aspects. In a now famous study, teachers were told that special testing revealed that some of their students were intellectually gifted. This information motivated teachers to treat these children as gifted, and many of them performed accordingly. Actually, the children were chosen at random.

The study clearly indicates that labeling, when believed, becomes a causative factor. A child often performs in a manner that justifies the label. What a simple way to dramatically improve not only educational, but career performance. The only ingredient that was present in the study, but is missing from our society, is the willingness to be generous.

Principle tells us that *everyone has the capacity to access Infinite Intelligence*. There are no limits placed on anyone at any time. All limits are self-imposed. The encouragement by the teacher stimulated and inspired the students to draw upon that Intelligence.

*The quality of each person's life is no better than it is because the individual will not permit it.* By our belief systems, often formed and reinforced in our early years, we place limits on how much joyfulness, peacefulness, and creativity we allow into our lives.

Change only occurs when there is a one-hundred-percent intention to bring it about. While it is true that at times change is self-initiated, it can easily be initiated by others. Teachers are in a perfect position to inspire such change.

When teachers are willing to label all children as gifted, the children will be encouraged to perceive themselves that way. Giftedness and talent have been generously bestowed upon everyone. They can be claimed at any time by those who are ready. The companion gift is joyfulness, our natural state of being. It is also ours for the claiming.

# CRIMINAL JUSTICE

Right and wrong, good and bad: these are the cornerstones of our society. This belief system created our criminal justice system with its police, prosecutors, judges, and prisoners—to name only a few of the participants in a vast system. This system costs several hundred billion dollars a year in the United States, yet crime continues to rise, recidivism is high, and there is a consensus that the system is not working well. Some believe it is too harsh; others believe it is too lenient.

Our criminal justice system is one of the most chaotic systems in our society and one of the most visible. Almost every television news program highlights recent crimes. Newspapers and magazines also feature them. For a topic that is so often addressed, it is very little understood. The statistics testify to that.

The universal principle that applies is nonjudgment— *there is no such thing as right and wrong, good and bad*. This principle is in direct contradiction to the belief system of the society. The chaos that exists is a result of the great distance between the two.

There has always been a strong commitment to the concept of right and wrong in our country, and punishment has been the remedy for wrongdoers. This practice is totally consistent with the underlying belief that when we separated ourselves from our Creator and each of us went his or her own way, our Creator became angry with us. The imagined guilt of this perceived transgression, not having been dealt with, is reenacted in our lives continually.

The criminal justice system is the mirror-image expression of our consciousness on the issue of judgment and guilt. As long as any of us individually—or most of us as a society—fails to make peace with God, the feeling of guilt remains, and the re-creation of the drama of crime and punishment continues.

There is a hidden cost in the retention of the belief in judgment of which most people are unaware. Principle tells us that *whenever we support the imprisonment of another, it imprisons us also.* In addition, the energy around any situation that we judge, freezes. It remains frozen until judgment is released. The discomfort that results is a signal from the Universe to look at the situation differently. Eventually, we come to the conclusion that judging anyone or anything is counterproductive. This is when the energy is freed and a sense of comfort and peacefulness is restored.

Prison inmates symbolize our belief in judgment and punishment. As we change this belief by feeling forgiveness growing into love for them, we come to feel love for all the other people against whom we are judgmental. Concurrently, we change the energy around the criminal justice system, which reflects the change by taking new form. Step by step, the existing system evolves into new forms that mirror the new belief system around judgment.

There is another aspect of the situation that requires understanding. We perceive inmates as the major actors in the drama, yet there are other groups that are equally important. These are the prison staff and all those who administer the criminal justice system.

While the system must change in response to our changed perception of the inmates, we can accelerate the process by our willingness to forgive the ones who participate in the administration of the system. These people have a vested interest in its continuation, for they perceive that their livelihoods depend upon it. Also, changing the system can be viewed by some of them as a judgment of their role by society. This group will require much love and support to facilitate the transition. However, they will be very grateful, for this support will free them, too.

When we forgive the staff, we forgive the part of ourselves that feels the need to be judgmental and to punish wrongdoing. When we forgive the inmates, we forgive the part of ourselves that we feel is guilty of unacceptable thoughts and behavior.

We can all look forward to the day when our release of judgment of everyone in our society brings new meaning to the experience of freedom.

# THOUGHT

Everyone has the capacity to think. We have tens of thousands of thoughts a day, and the ways we may combine them or relate to them are infinite. Great rewards are given for thinking in certain ways. Doctors, lawyers, executives, scientists, and many others are rewarded for thinking as they do. College education—a training in disciplined thinking—is highly valued and is an entrance requirement to many of the preferred positions in our society.

Much has been written recently about the power of thought. We are told that our thoughts create our reality. If I think you are an honest person, I trust you. If I think a particular food is detrimental to my health, I avoid it. What is the effect of all of this thinking, and how does it relate to universal principles?

There are two categories of thought. One uses the conscious mind and occurs when we figure something out. Society favors this approach, which encourages us to "think before we act."

The other category is usually overlooked. It is the thought that emanates from the Infinite Intelligence that created us. This kind of thought is always available to us. It is commonly referred to as intuition. Whether or not we use it is always our choice. Since society promotes conscious-mind thinking, our tendency is to favor it. The educational system and most other institutions in our society reinforce this choice.

Intuition is accessed only when we allow the conscious-mind process to recede. A hallmark of our intuition, the knowingness that comes to us, is its preference for quiet. As long as we are engaged in conscious-mind activity, we do not hear it or feel it.

In our society, intuition is perceived as a process that is more natural to women. While men may use it, they do not talk about it very much, and it is certainly not encouraged among men.

Society offers substantial rewards for use of the conscious mind. Thus, those who are receiving these rewards and those who hope to receive them have a vested interest in favoring the conscious mind over an alternative that is freely available.

Accessing Infinite Intelligence is a fascinating process. It forces us to deal with the very issues that block the experience of our inner joyfulness. In the process of quieting down the conscious mind, so that we can hear and feel our intuition, we surrender our perception of difference, inequality, and attachment to materialism. We settle into a *feeling* of Oneness with the Universe and all of Its components.

# EMOTION

What is the relationship between feeling and emotion? Emotion is the attachment of a thought to a feeling. Thoughts naturally flow through our minds, and feelings through our bodies. The attachment creates an energy block that is felt as discomfort.

Feelings are a basic currency of the human condition. Everyone has them, and each of us is capable of experiencing an infinite variety of feelings. They are like colors. There are not only many colors, there are many shades and combinations of them. One color is not more important than another. Red is not more valuable than green, blue is not more beautiful than yellow. It is marvelous to have many colors in our environment and experience the ways in which they enhance our lives, from paintings and decorations to sunrises and sunsets.

The problem arises when we introduce the conscious mind into the experience. As soon as we judge, evaluate, or describe the way we feel about something, we distort our natural response to it. We also create an energy block.

Contrary to what we are taught, *life is a feeling experience that is inherently joyful.* We allow ourselves to feel it when we open ourselves to giving and receiving unconditional love. How simple the process is! How natural it is! Yet we seem to avoid it at every opportunity.

The concept of emotion derives from this avoidance. It puts a premium on distorting and blocking joyfulness by encouraging us to believe that our thoughts about our feelings are accurate and absolute. Invariably, we interpret feelings in terms of the circumstances around which they occur. When we are at a funeral, we describe our feelings as sadness or grief. When we are threatened physically, we describe our feelings as fear. When we are isolated

69

from others, we describe our feelings as loneliness. When we are sexually aroused, we describe our feelings as passion.

Our ability to analyze, label, and interpret feelings is limitless. Each time we do it, we distort the basic quality of the experience. We also create an energy block within us that we experience as discomfort. It is the Universe's way of encouraging us to release the thought that we have attached to the feeling.

Freed of our conscious-mind intervention, we experience an infinite range of feelings. There is a simple way to release the discomfort that comes from attaching a thought to a feeling. It is to open our hearts, feel the love that is there, and then embrace the emotion—fear, anger or grief. This enables us to integrate the feeling within us, free of the thoughts we have about it.

We are feeling beings. Sometimes the feelings are very intense. We learned, inaccurately, that in order to feel intensely, we must be responding to a dramatic circumstance. The truth is that we can feel intensely just for the fun of it.

When we open our hearts and embrace every situation with love, the intensity of the feeling remains without the discomfort caused by the drama.

The feelings we have at weddings and funerals, or at hearing reports of murder and rape, are all perfect just the way they are. It is self-supportive to feel these feelings fully and embrace them as part of us. In opening ourselves to these feelings, we reclaim the parts of ourselves that we previously disowned. We are here to experience all of ourselves. What a joy it is to open ourselves to all that we are capable of feeling!

Joyfulness has a partner. It is peacefulness. To feel joyfulness, we must be in a state of peacefulness. This means we have released all need to judge anything or feel attached to it. It is a state of being in which we trust the Universe as a place of total support and safety. We truly feel that the Universe unconditionally loves and supports us just the way we are. This absence of all resistance to allowing the present moment to be perfect opens us to feeling our Oneness with all.

Having addressed thoughts and feelings, I feel that it is essential to clarify their relative importance.

Conscious-mind thinking is the way we generally support our separation from each other. The conscious mind is the vehicle that makes up and then focuses on all the ways we are different. The conscious mind has been trained to believe that the differences among us are real and necessary, that the world is an unsafe place, and that we have to protect ourselves from one another. This produces a great deal of chaos. However, chaos is all an illusion. Once we feel our connnectedness with others, fear and chaos recede.

The power of the conscious mind is in its willingness to choose to align with the Universe. There is no power in the Universe apart from the Intelligence that created It. When we join in partnership with It, we experience real power and true creativity.

What is creativity? It is the continual expansion of every thing and every entity that emanates from our Source. Each of us, having been created by Infinite Intelligence, has the power to expand that part of us that is God substance. This is our Essence, our Soul. It endures forever and is not subject to change by our conscious mind. It is inherently perfect. As our connection with the Intelligence that created us, our Soul is a source of guidance for us. It inspires us to proceed in ways that join with each other and with our Source.

Each of us is a unique expression of the creativity of God. The talents given us are the ways we creatively express ourselves in partnership with the Source of the talent. What is not commonly understood is that there are an infinite number of ways for us to express ourselves in alignment with the Universe. These expressions are always fulfilling and are always supportive of ourselves and of everything in the Universe. They sustain feelings of joyfulness and peacefulness that keep expanding as we allow ourselves to feel them more and more.

Most of us fail to appreciate the power of our feelings. *How we feel about anything determines the way we experience it.* When the feeling is joyfulness, in any of its myriad forms, it attracts more joy. This inspires even more creative expression on the part of those feeling the joyfulness.

71

There is no limit to our creativity. There is no limit to our joyfulness. There is no limit to the ways we can creatively join with one another and play together.

# ANGER, GRIEF AND OTHER EMOTIONS

Principle tells us that if I feel anger from you, it must be reflecting something inside of me. In other words, a part of me must be angry, in order for me to feel that anger in your presence. It is not your behavior that causes the anger, since not everyone would respond with anger to your actions. It is only felt by a person who is resonating with the anger as a projection of his own energy and perception.

The solution to feeling the discomfort of anger and other emotions, such as anxiety and grief, is to recognize that each so-called emotion is a judgment attached to a feeling, and that the judgment belongs to us. There is a purpose in attracting people to us who reflect our judgments back to us. It is the only practical way in which we can discover what we keep buried inside of us.

If you were to ask an angry person the cause of his anger, he would invariably blame someone or something. It is to reverse this misperception that we keep creating the opportunity for the reversal.

The same Entity that created life built in the mechanisms to support it. The principle of free will allows us to choose to see this same situation in a way that is helpful rather than painful. Once we recognize the true dynamics of a situation, we can embark upon a process of viewing it differently. When the recognition occurs together with the intention to change, a major energy block is released. Though it will still take commitment to complete the process, a noticeable improvement in the quality of one's life occurs.

Making peace with our emotions requires only the willingness to love them just the way they are. We do this by embracing the emotion, whether it be anxiety or grief, with love. We incorporate the emotion lovingly within us and accept it as part of us.

Our hearts dissolve judgments, and all that is left is the pure feeling. What enters our hearts as anger, grief, or anxiety becomes a vibration that feels wonderful just the way it is.

Whenever we embrace someone or something in our hearts, we end our sense of separation from the person or thing. It is an act of expanding our consciousness that eliminates a source of difference, competition, or challenge. This, in turn, simplifies our lives.

Keeping the sense of separation alive requires effort. It is a draining and weakening approach to life. Embracing and incorporating releases resistance. It frees our energy and is felt as aliveness, exuberance, and a zest for life.

As more of us do this, we come to appreciate the true meaning of Oneness. Feeling our Oneness can be as intense an experience as we wish. It teaches us that it is a gross misperception to believe that we require events and circumstances outside of us to bring about intense feelings.

It is clear that each of us, at times, wishes to experience intense feelings. We can now relax in the knowledge that crises, competitions, and all of our adversarial ways of relating to one another are not only unnecessary, they are poor substitutes for the intense feeling of joy, which we can open to whenever we choose.

Joy is our birthright. Joy is our natural state of being. The more we share it, the more intense it becomes.

There is no inherent limit to our ability to feel joy—in all its aspects, intensities, and colors—all the time.

We are entering an era of learning how to feel love, deeply and without drama. We can, in perfect quiet, or in any other setting, feel the intensity of our feelings, which are just vibrations. These vibrations have an infinite range. One is not better than another. The variety of them adds richly to the feeling quality of our lives. And each vibration is an expression of our joyfulness—the only real feeling we ever have.

# EXCITEMENT

Excitement is stimulation created by a circumstance outside of ourselves. It can be the competition of playing poker, the uncertainty of investing in the stock market, the tension of meeting monthly living expenses, or the suspense of reading fiction or watching a movie. We are constantly encouraged to seek excitement out. So insidious is the message that unless an activity creates tension, it seems unsatisfying. It is no wonder that the achievement of inner peace is a rare occurrence.

What, then, can possibly be the lure of peacefulness? It is a craving of our Souls. It is a deep longing that pushes upward relentlessly. We do not have to create peacefulness. We need only relinquish our fascination with something else.

Tension derives from fear which is based on our belief that we really separated from our Source. Tension-producing activities are a natural consequence of a society based on separation. On our own, life *is* scary.

The assumption of most people is that without excitement life is not worth living. We perceive that the opposite of excitement is boredom, a circumstance that is totally unacceptable. Our conception of boredom is inaccurate. It is not the absence of excitement. It is another phase of it. We are bored when we perceive that we need excitement and do not have it. This leads us to create excitement over and over again. Excitement is always outer-directed. We rely on someone or something outside of ourselves to stimulate us—a ballgame, an argument, or an award.

Let us examine excitement and inner peace by looking at the qualities associated with each. Excitement generates bravado, competition, and concern for image. These qualities are temporary and unstable. Inner peace gives rise to joyfulness, mutual support, and a recognition of our own divinity. The qualities it supports are enduring and steady. Excitement is not natural; inner peace is.

In addition to being our natural state, peacefulness is the context for real creativity. Creativity is a partnership. It is a conscious joining of ourselves with the Universe in the expression of our talents. It is the awareness of Oneness and an opening to the endless flow of universal energy. This energy seeks expansion and provides a sense of fulfillment for everyone who opens to it.

There is no limit to the creativity each of us can express when we open to the inspiration of universal energy. There are an infinite number of ways that sounds can be joined in music, colors and shapes can be combined in visual art, ideas can be interrelated in inspiring projects, and people can be united in harmonious forms of community.

Inner peace is not boring. It is a state of being that opens us to the heartfelt qualities we treasure the most: the tender love of a mother for her newborn child; the deep satisfaction from expressing a talent fully and freely; the joy of helping a person in need; the profound sense of safety and security from feeling at One with the Universe and with others.

# HONESTY

Telling the truth is one of our greatest challenges. As children, we receive the message from our parents and other adults that honesty is not always appreciated. We also learn that most adults have a double standard when it comes to honesty. This mirrors the society's belief that it is foolish to tell the truth under all circumstances.

In negotiations, it is customary for one party to demand more than he expects and for the other to offer less than he knows he is willing to pay. In response to children's questions, parents often answer evasively, to avoid dealing with subjects that are uncomfortable. Most of us do not respond honestly when asked, "How are you?"

Our pattern of not telling the truth to each other encourages us not to tell the truth to ourselves. Since there is no right and wrong, honesty is really a different issue from what we believe it to be.

One of the most self-destructive attitudes we can adopt is not being honest with ourselves. Many of us have lost touch with who we really are, how we really feel, and what we really wish. The trip back to self-understanding can be long and demanding; yet it is one of the most important and meaningful trips we ever take.

During the transitional period of finding out who we really are and learning to love ourselves, we often have to respond to circumstances that present seemingly tough choices. For example, many of us who have created financial obligations as a reflection of our own self-demanding natures, face creditors who seem demanding. Others of us who have entered into relationships that are not harmonious find ourselves having to release judgment of people who reflect our own hidden conflicts.

Since right and wrong are not valid guidelines, what is truth? Truth, for each of us, is a personal experience. It is an awareness of what we feel in the present moment, without judgment. We have to learn that every request and every denial of a request can be made lovingly.

The apparent degree of difficulty in feeling love under varying circumstances is only a perceptual difference. Once we are willing to open to the love within us, we realize that it is no more difficult to feel love for a demanding creditor or a tyrant than for a friend.

Another aspect of honesty is being at peace with what feels perfect under the circumstances, even though we might perceive it as judgmental. Acting indignantly can be perfect—if that is how we really feel. It is important to honor our true feelings instead of the feelings we believe we ought to have.

We have created what appears to be a complex society as a reflection of our confused consciousness. Gaining clarity requires patience and perseverance with ourselves and with each other. We eventually recognize that love is indivisible. It is not more difficult in one situation than in another.

Another challenge in being honest is learning to say no in a loving manner. Many people undertake obligations and accede to others' requests out of an inability to say no.

Often, saying no is the most loving way to respond. Children regularly look to parents to set limits for them. There are parents who have difficulty expressing love for their children. They either say no in an unloving manner or say yes when they really wish to say no.

Saying no is not the issue. What really matters is feeling love for the person to whom we are responding. When we feel loving, we respond appropriately.

When we say no to another person in a loving way, we say yes to ourselves. It is a way of honoring what we believe, and it is a clear statement of our willingness to love ourselves.

# OBLIGATION

What a premium we place on obligation! It is one of the dominant motivations of many people in our society. Parents do much for children out of a sense of obligation. Children often feel obligated to act in expected ways toward their parents. Our decision to borrow freely to buy houses, cars, and other items has placed almost everyone in a position of obligation toward insurance companies, department stores, banks, and other lending institutions. Our system of taxation creates obligations to our federal, state, and local governments. Even marriage places the bride and groom in a position of obligation to each other.

It is fair to say that our society has a strong obligation and debt consciousness. These obligations invariably create much discomfort. Generally speaking, parent-child relationships are less than wonderful; defaults on loans, and the lawsuits that derive from them, are at an all-time high, and increasing; resistance to paying taxes is considered normal; and divorces are occuring at an average annual rate of 50 percent.

When we look at principle, we gain insight into the creation and expansion of our obligation and debt consciousness. Each of us, in our connection to the Infinite Intelligence that created us, knows what life is all about. Most of the time we suppress or avoid this knowledge, but it is always there. On a subconscious level we know precisely what the motivation is for another person's behavior.

When a parent acts out of a sense of obligation toward her child, the child knows it. When a child acts out of a sense of obligation toward her parent, the parent knows it. Husbands and wives know when their spouses are acting out of a sense of obligation, regardless of what is outwardly said or done. No one ever fools anyone else, yet we seem to have an unwritten agreement to make believe we really do not know the underlying motivation.

There are other principles that influence our attitude toward obligation. The first is honesty. Many of us believe that it is not safe to tell the truth to each other. Guided by this belief, parents often hide the truth from their children, who in turn do the same to their parents. Government officials commonly hide the truth from the citizens they serve.

Though our behavior patterns are often slanted toward avoiding honesty, we gain trust for someone only when we feel the person is honest with us. We crave honesty, and yet we encourage others to withhold it from us.

Honesty leads to trust, and trust leads to opening ourselves to our basic desire to give and receive unconditional love. The models of behavior we have developed in our society promote lack of trust. They reflect the basic distrust we have for our Creator.

As we surrender to each other and feel the unconditional love that is within each of us, we are releasing distrust for our Creator. Each relationship mirrors the other. We are learning to make peace with our Creator by living in peace with each other. It is a beautiful process that is most fulfilling, and everyone can participate.

As was stated earlier, pain is self-created and is always the outer manifestation of fear. Fear is always a withholding of love. It is a personal choice, which we may choose to reverse at any moment. We desperately wish to connect with one another, and too often we have created that connection through obligation. Consistent with our other adversarial approaches, we have established the way we relate to each other in a pain-creating manner.

Pain is one of the greatest illusions. We do so much to alleviate pain. Yet the only approach that truly relieves it is the willingness to give and receive love in those instances where we previously withheld it. Once we recognize that we really love our creditors, parents, children, and spouses, we can experience the same connection joyfully rather than painfully.

The concept of Oneness tells us that whenever we feel love for anyone or anything, it represents feeling love for everyone and everything. Love is truly indivisible. When we are able to totally and completely love one person unconditionally, it means we love everyone unconditionally.

Unconditional love means a total release of all judgment toward everyone, including ourselves and our Creator. It means we have, on a feeling level, totally forgiven everyone for everything.

Remember that every step taken in the direction of feeling more love is supported by the Universe. Enjoying the process ensures our commitment to continue feeling more love through releasing more judgment and forgiving more. When each step is anticipated eagerly, we know a successful outcome is assured.

The Universe is a model of freedom—free choice, free expression of unconditional love and support, free feelings of joy and inner peace. When we totally trust the Universe, truly believe It is always unconditionally loving and supportive, we release our connection with one another through obligation. We recognize that all we are capable of is loving each other. It is what we ultimately surrender to, and that means total freedom.

# PATRIOTISM

Patriotism is a complex concept. It is presented and taught as love of country. Yet true love is unconditional and indivisible. We cannot love our own country and hate another.

A common patriotic belief is that we must support our country's actions whether they are right or wrong. This raises another contradiction. If we perceive our country as functioning in ways that can be either right or wrong, then we are judging it, and whenever we judge anything, we are incapable of truly loving it.

Patriotism, under the guise of being a concept that guides us and models a beneficial pattern of behavior, is really a concept that mirrors the contradictions and misperceptions that are the hallmarks of the world of illusion.

Principle is Oneness, and Oneness is indivisible. As we allow ourselves to unconditionally love the people we know, we find it easier to feel that love for strangers. Everyone is worthy of love, regardless of his outward behavior or political preference.

The solution to international conflict is first forgiving and then feeling love for those whom we presently perceive as having interests inimical to ours or acting in ways that are distasteful to us.

The solution is always the same. Underneath everyone's outer behavior is a need to give and receive love. Whenever we respond to the emotion of a situation, we deepen the misperceptions in our own consciousness and in the consciousness of any others who are involved. When we are able to see through or beyond the emotion, to the Essence of the individual, we feel our Oneness with him. This empowers him to express who he really is.

We always have a choice either to empower the illusion—the misperception—or to empower our clarity. No matter what our choice was a moment ago, we are free to choose again in the present moment. In truth, all prior choices are released into our present choice.

Whenever we choose to honor the Essence of another, it is as though we never accepted the illusion. Whenever we choose forgiveness and love, it dissolves guilt. We recognize that we never did anything wrong in the first place, and eventually we recognize that we were never really capable of anything but unconditional love.

Patriotism is a useful concept to the extent that it brings people together and helps them bond with one another. It is not useful in the ways that it encourages separation from others. We are now ready to release models that discourage us from seeing beyond the illusion. We are now ready to see the Essence in everyone and to invite *everyone* to play with us.

# DEMOCRACY

Democracy, as it is currently practiced in the United States, recognizes the ways in which each of us is different. These differences are often promoted by specific interest groups. Thus, there are groups promoting women's rights, minority rights, gay rights, and states' rights, to name a few.

These competing interests are kept in balance by our federal system of government. Using the power of the vote, interest groups encourage legislators to pass laws and attempt to have executives (presidents, governors, and mayors) use the authority of their offices to favor their respective interests.

Partly in response to these groups and also as a result of differing political and economic philosophies, there are two or more parties seeking election. This ensures continual competition, not only at election time, but also during the periods in between.

To compound the foregoing, there is continual competition within the parties between liberal and conservative blocs, and even among candidates with similar views.

It is interesting to note how competition within the political process mirrors the competition within the larger society.

Civilization is an evolutionary experience. Democracy is a rather advanced form of government. In taking rights from rulers with arbitrary powers and giving them to an electorate, a great improvement was made. It is now time to look at the next step in the process.

Principle tells us that the ways in which we are different from one another are not significant. We see the differences in each other because we feel different from each other. By accentuating differences, we reinforce our underlying belief that we are separate from the Intelligence that created us.

We shall continue to focus on the differences among us as long as we avoid dealing with the underlying issue of equality. It is ironic that many minority groups perceive that they obtain an advantage by furthering the ways in which they are different.

In all essential ways, we are alike. Everyone craves unconditional love and support. As society offers unconditional love and support as a model of choice, more and more people will be attracted to it.

We are just beginning to be aware of the stifling effect of competitiveness and the freeing nature of a supportive and accepting environment. We have barely begun to appreciate the extraordinary and unique talents that lie buried in each of us. Understanding and valuing the ways we can encourage the expression of these talents allows us to blend and to harmonize them into marvelous new products and services that support and expand peace and harmony on the planet.

*A significant part of the process is feeling unconditional love and support for those who resist or feel threatened by the shift.* In order for the shift to be successful, everyone must be given unconditional love, whether he agrees with the change or not.

It is important to understand what the true shift is. It is a shift from viewing life as primarily a rational or thinking experience to viewing it as a feeling experience.

There is only one energy in the Universe and it is love. The feeling quality that accompanies love is joyfulness. Whenever we open our hearts, we feel joyfulness in one of its infinite varieties.

Democracy is a system that allows us to choose. It is time to choose unconditional love and its companion—joy.

# JUSTICE

Justice is one of the concepts upon which our society is based. It connotes fairness and evenhandedness. The institution for determining whether or not justice is done is the court system. In other words, judges preside over the dispensing of justice. Their opinions and decisions guide the rest of us in our behavior toward one another.

What is most interesting about the process is that it is fraught with disagreement. Many of the decisions made by higher courts, where more than one judge presides, contain dissenting opinions. In matters before individual judges, the disparity of opinion and decision in similar situations is remarkable for its inconsistency. In summary, justice in our society is very uncertain.

It is important to appreciate how uncomfortable this uncertainty makes us feel. For the average person, the thought of going to court brings fear and often great anxiety. Isn't this a strange way to feel about an institution that was established to support us?

Judges and the court system are generally viewed as problem solvers. The dilemma that the system generates for its citizens is understood when we look at how the system solves a problem. The method used accepts the validity of the beliefs that people have conflicting interests and there must be a winner and a loser. Thus, the true resolution of the problem is not achieved.

For example, two businessmen enter into a contract to buy and sell grain. Between the time of contract and the delivery date, major changes occur in the grain market. The price of grain rises sharply; at the same time there is a shortage of labor to harvest the grain. If the party selling the grain pays a premium to attract laborers to harvest the grain, he loses a substantial sum of money. The contract does not take these sudden and extreme changes in the marketplace into account. The buyer, eager to enjoy a huge wind-fall profit, insists on delivery at the agreed price. The seller goes to court for relief.

The assumptions of the buyer are:

He was smart enough or lucky enough to make an advantageous contract;

Since business involves competition, some win and some lose;

His survival in business depends on his ability to win more often than he loses;

Other businessmen are using the same guidelines.

The results that flow from following these assumptions are often uncomfortable for both parties. In the example offered, the time, energy, and financial cost of litigating the dispute is substantial. Even the successful party loses a great deal.

Principle provides entirely different guidelines. The assumptions underlying them are:

There is more than enough for everyone, since abundance is the natural state of affairs in the Universe.

Being generous benefits the giver as much as it does the receiver.

Since we are all connected, when we support each other, everyone feels better.

When I treat another lovingly, I am really expressing love for myself.

Using these guidelines, businessmen are naturally supportive of each other. In the example given, the buyer and seller can easily adjust the price to reflect the unexpected changes in the market-place. In this way both businessmen become winners and feel the joy of mutual support.

The businessman who disregards the truth that the Universe is a place of abundance for all, who sees an advantage in creating loss for another, and who sees himself as separate from the other businessman, feels the pain of withholding his love and support

90

from his brother. He also denies himself the joy of expressing his generosity.

Whether or not to use principle to resolve the situation is a matter of free will and free choice for the participants. Principle accords everyone the freedom to make any decision he wishes. Principle does not, however, grant the power to control the consequences that flow from the decision. Consequences are mandated at the universal level.

Thus, if I choose to make money the primary consideration in a transaction, I receive the consequences of that choice, which is always discomfort. It is the signal from the Universe to choose again.

Life is a big classroom. The Universe is the teacher. We can choose any lesson we wish to learn. The Universe always guides us to the most appropriate solution.

Within each of us is the need to be loving and supportive of ourselves and others. This is basic to the human condition. However, many of us have interpreted life quite differently. We have taught ourselves, rigorously, that life is adversarial and competitive.

Since this belief is not natural to us, it requires continual reaffirmation to keep it alive. For many people, the commitment to keep it alive is so strong that they continually block and suppress their true underlying feelings.

Our commitment to deny who we really are exacts a heavy price. Justice cannot work as it is presently dispensed. It violates principle. It attempts to solve problems using the same misconceptions that created them in the first place.

The Universe is a marvelous teacher. It is patient and consistent. People who use principle in their lives gain the benefit. Those who do not are continually signaled to change their approach.

# ORGANIZED RELIGION

The basic approach of the dominant Western religions is that people's behavior is either good or bad. This is implemented by various religious rules and regulations that carry the penalty of punishment by the Deity if the rules are broken. Anyone adhering to one of these systems has some fear of the Deity. This fear supports most people's belief that God is not always loving and supportive.

The universal principle that applies is nonjudgment. There is no standard such as good and bad or right and wrong. All behavior flows from a person's perception. When we perceive someone as loving and lovable regardless of his behavior, we respond by being loving and supportive. When we perceive someone as unloving, we often respond by being unloving in return.

Anyone who truly believes, at a deep feeling level, that God is a loving Entity under *all* circumstances will see his fellow man the same way. Thus he will, with total certainty and consistency, offer loving support to everyone.

Conceptually, it is all very simple. However, bridging the gap between the larger society's commitment to right and wrong and the universal principle of nonjudgment is a monumental challenge. It requires not only the deepest commitment but also the constant support of friends with similar intentions.

While individuals, groups, and institutions—including organized religions—are in disagreement on many issues, there is a great deal of agreement on the issue of right, wrong, and punishment. In order for our society and all others to reach a state of harmony and togetherness within themselves and with each other, there will first have to be an acceptance of this principle of nonjudgment.

Hopefully, acceptance of this principle will be encouraged by the creation and demonstration of a true brotherhood, across all religious lines, fostered by the leadership of the organized religions.

# FAILURE

Failure is the belief that in some way we are not good enough to be loved unconditionally, just the way we are. People who perceive themselves as failures, as well as those who are afraid to fail, are motivated by the same belief: I am not loved just the way I am.

There is a need in everyone to express and to receive love. This need is repressed by people who believe that it is not safe to give and receive love freely. If we believe there are circumstances under which love will be withheld from us, we pattern our behavior to accommodate this belief.

Children are trained by parents who give or withhold love as a way of inducing the children to accept the parents' beliefs. Parents, as authority figures, mirror their own beliefs about the ultimate authority figure—God. Parents who believe that God is not always unconditionally loving will at times act in unloving ways toward their children.

Principle supports us by reflecting our beliefs back to us so that we can take another look at them. Eventually, awareness of the process leads us to change our beliefs. The only circumstance under which we allow ourselves to love everyone unconditionally is when we believe that it is totally safe to do so. Feeling that degree of safety emanates from the new belief: No one is capable of taking anything that is real away from us, particularly life itself. In truth, we cannot fail, except by insisting that failure is real.

# HELPLESSNESS

There are many times when we feel helpless. People with no mechanical skills often feel helpless when mechanical objects stop operating. A recently divorced mother left with small children and no financial support may feel helpless. Illness can create a feeling of helplessness, as can unemployment. Hurricanes and earthquakes may leave us feeling helpless as well.

Each of the foregoing situations involves a response to an event in the physical world. Principle tells us that our experiences with the physical world are of our own making. They mirror the state of our consciousness. Helplessness is a result of seeking lasting help where it is impossible to find it—in the world outside of us.

The feeling of helplessness is an accurate perception when relying on the physical world for support. In fact, it is useful as a way of encouraging us to look elsewhere. Eventually, we come to the realization that we must look within.

In those moments when we surrender in consciousness to the helplessness, we are able to go beyond it. That is when we feel the peace within. Outer events or circumstances lose their importance and their power.

Solutions to the problems of life come from insight. Insight is the way in which Infinite Intelligence talks to us. When we use our conscious minds to devise a solution and then try to bring it about, we fail to hear the suggestion from our inner guidance.

The willingness to surrender to helplessness is a big step forward. It leads us to release our reliance on solutions that are temporary at best. It is only when we release our dependence on money and the material world that we experience the abundance of the Universe. It is only when we release judgment that we understand what perfection* means. It is only through the release of the conscious mind that we find out what Infinite Intelligence is. It is only through the release of effort and struggle—making things happen—that we find out what ease and simplicity are. It is only when we learn to surrender to others that we experience what unconditional love is.

The choices are always available. Our inner knowingness keeps us moving to the cutting edge of our lives—the place where we discover what we are ready to learn. When we trust the process and surrender to it, understanding becomes easier. As we learn to join together in support of one another, the process becomes fun. Remember, life is really an experience in consciousness. Pain is self-created and can only be released from within. Joy is our natural state, waiting patiently to be reclaimed.

# POVERTY, DISEASE, AND FORGIVENESS

We look around the world and see millions of people who live in various states of poverty. There are even many people experiencing poverty in countries like the United States, which is considered a wealthy country.

In noticing extreme conditions such as poverty, we often perceive that the person in the extreme circumstance is experiencing much pain. The pain seems to be transferred empathically to the individual desiring to alter the pain-creating circumstance.

For an observer who is eager to eliminate it, poverty appears to be the most painful experience. For a person trying to eradicate cancer, that disease seems to be the most painful circumstance. A closer look tells us that pain exists in every element of society. Is it fair to say that a wealthy person in the final stages of a degenerative disease suffers less pain than an impoverished one? People at all economic levels resort to drugs and alcohol to dull their pain. Some even end their lives to eliminate the pain.

Let us look at pain. *It is a manifestation in the physical body of fear, which is a withholding of love.* Pain is always self-created from within. The mirror principle tells us that we *experience around us a reenactment of the state of our consciousness.* Pain is one of the images we mirror for each other. A shift to less pain occurs when we choose to express love rather than withhold it. This means feeling forgiveness for the people in our lives from whom we previously withheld forgiveness and love.

The demonstration of pain is always a choice. The choice may have been made many years previously and under circumstances that have long since been forgotten. Nevertheless, the principle of free will always applies.

While it is possible to release a misperception in an instant, and thus release the pain caused by that misperception, it usually takes a period of time to totally forgive people against whom we hold deep resentments and anger.

Every time any person feels forgiveness, that moment prepares the way for others to follow. There are so many people focusing on the process of forgiveness at the present time that it is becoming progressively easier for all of us who enter into the process. Remember, we are all connected in essential ways. Movement by anyone toward alignment with the Universe benefits all of us.

When a person who is in pain requests support, it is proper to respond in any way that feels appropriate. The response can be feeding the hungry, offering medical assistance to the ill, or encouraging tyrants to release political prisoners.

The support need not end there. Whenever there is receptivity, it is helpful to encourage the person experiencing pain to change his perception. This support is best offered by people who demonstrate the power of inner peace, forgiveness, and love by their presence.

Remember, tyrants, criminals, and racists are also entitled to forgiveness and unconditional love. They are mirroring the consciousness of those of us who are still holding on to similar beliefs, though possibly in lesser amounts. We are truly in this game of life together. Although it often does not appear that way, we are most helpful to each other when we improve the quality of our own lives. The simple act of demonstrating the joy of living our lives according to universal principles inspires others to follow.

# POLLUTION

We recognize the damage to our environment from pollution. This recognition has led to the creation of federal, state, and local environmental protection agencies. Yet, according to the evidence, the problem seems to be outpacing attempts to control it. The quality of drinking water keeps declining, cities and villages are running out of garbage landfills, and nuclear wastes are growing although no one seems to have any understanding of how to detoxify or safely store them. These are just the beginning of a long list.

Pollution illustrates one of many problems that seem to have gone out of control in our society.

The first step in dealing with such a circumstance is to make peace with it. Becoming angry, depressed, or discouraged are just different ways of expressing judgment. Responding in this way keeps the energy frozen around the troubling situation. In order to free energy so that change can occur, we must release all of our judgments, not only of the situation but also of the people involved in the situation. For example, we must forgive executives of companies that create nuclear and other toxic wastes, developers who replace grass and trees with blacktop, and officials who order the spraying of Agent Orange. We must also forgive those who wish to stop the polluters. Whatever they are inspired to do is perfect also.

Feeling forgiveness means ending the sense of separation we feel from one another. When we embrace polluters, we empower the part of them that feels their connectedness to everyone. They begin to realize that disregard of the environment or of others is an act of violence against themselves.

The final step is the surprising one. It requires releasing attachment to correcting the perceived problem and lovingly embracing

101

the situation and all participants—polluters and antipolluters—just the way they are.

All problems are an outplaying of the state of our consciousness. The temptation is to fix the outer condition— somehow stop the polluters. Principle tells us that *opposing something energizes it as much as supporting it does.* The result is opposite to what we seem to want. When we lovingly embrace that which troubles us, we support the resolution of the situation in a way that benefits everyone. Our hearts can compose and harmonize apparent differences in ways that our minds cannot.

Understanding comes from appreciating the true causative element in the Universe. Conscious-mind solutions just create more illusions. We cannot solve one illusion with another. The inner knowing of each of us, and of all of us together, contains the insight for the solution. True solutions result from changes in consciousness. Making peace with the situation, releasing all judgment about it and embracing it with love allows a solution to emerge. The solution is invariably an inspiration that harmoniously joins previously competing interests.

The ultimate resolution of the challenge of pollution occurs with the recognition of our Oneness and our commitment to honor this Oneness in the face of evidence that seems to prove its nonexistence.

# WORK AND EFFORT

We work to pass school examinations and to succeed at careers. We work to master a sport such as baseball, tennis, or golf. We even work when we learn to dance, speak in public, and become better husbands, wives, and parents.

It seems that we only value an accomplishment if we have to work to achieve it. This is at variance with principle. The Universe, including each of us, is whole and complete just the way It is. Our unwillingness to believe this creates the need for work or effort.

Work results from trying to improve a situation that is perceived to be less than perfect just the way it is. If I believe I have to earn a living, I start preparing myself for a life of work at an early age. Watching my parents and other parents work hard leads me to assume there is no other way.

It is much like believing that the Earth is flat and therefore not venturing far from home for fear of falling off the edge. When Columbus looked at the situation differently and acted accordingly, people's perceptions changed. As a way to view working or any other effort differently, let us assume that along with the gift of life comes total support for a life of ease and joy. We know that when we act lovingly in support of one another, life is easy and joyful. Doing the same thing out of love, that we did previously out of need totally changes the experience.

It is our unwillingness to feel love for ourselves and each other that is the basis for our perceived need to work hard and to resist the natural order. When we love *ourselves*, we allow ourselves to ask others for support. When we love *others*, we allow them to support us. We know in our hearts that giving and receiving are the same, and the giver is really giving a gift to himself.

Abundance flows in our lives only when we release our resistance to it. Our resistance manifests itself when we withhold love from ourselves and others. We are free to reverse the process whenever we are ready.

Life is truly a perceptual experience. The way we perceive it is the way we experience it. A life of ease, joy, peace, and abundance is our birthright. It is ours to receive and share lovingly with our brothers and sisters. The only price is surrender to the truth of who we really are and what life is truly all about.

# PLANNING AND DECISION MAKING

Teachers have lesson plans. Executives have business plans. Athletes have game plans. Individuals have daily plans. We are a society of planners.

Planning and decision making arise from the belief that each of us or a group of us can choose from all of the variables involved in a particular situation. We decide which are desirable and the best way to achieve them. Planning and decision making are considered to be a demonstration of intelligence—a typical way in which we use our conscious minds.

Principle helps us to view the conscious mind or individual intelligence in relationship to universal Mind or Infinite Intelligence. What is the difference in function and result?

Conscious-mind intelligence is limited by facts, information, experiences, and all of the ways an individual or group of individuals can accumulate and organize information. No matter how brilliant the individual or the members of a group, it is impossible for them to be aware of all of the variables, facts, options, and opportunities available in the Universe.

Infinite Intelligence has access to all of the factors involved in every situation. Through our intuition, each of us can have the benefit of this total knowledge. Therefore, decision making and planning, as it is customarily practiced, is not the most effective way to proceed.

Does this mean that no one can ever plan ahead? Sometimes it is appropriate to make a decision in the present for something that will occur in the future. However it is preferable to use intuition, our connection with Infinite Intelligence as the basis of whether or not to make the decision and any arrangements in connection with it.

In universal terms,* linear time does not exist. Our conscious minds perceive the future by relating it only to the past. Yet everything exists only in the present. Our knowingness, our connection to Infinite Intelligence, guides us in the present with certainty and ease.

We are once again faced with a choice of belief systems. The result always derives from the system we have chosen. In our society we generally select the tangible alternative. Yet it is the intangible one, the one based on trust, that offers the greatest reward.

# COMPETITION

We compete for jobs, parts in a play, positions on a team, and political office. We compete for a job in a company so that we can compete with other companies. We compete for a position on a team so that we can compete with other teams.

As citizens we are taught to feel competitive toward other countries. As members of a particular faith or religion we feel competitive toward other faiths and religions. Ours is a most competitive society.

From the standpoint of principle, there is no such thing as competition. We all come from the same Source and we are all equal. The differences we perceive and feel the need to emphasize grow out of our commitment to forget who we really are.

In our hearts we know our differences are superficial. We naturally feel compassion for each other.

Competition is the result of a choice to continue the illusion that we are separate from each other. We know that when we participate in an activity that is unloving, not only is the so-called loser hurt but the winner as well. Either everyone wins or no one wins.

One of the ways we justify the use of competition is the claim that it will raise the skill and performance level of the participants. As a teacher of tennis, using universal principles both in the instruction and as the basis for the play, I can attest to the fact that the performance of the participants improves much faster in a supportive, rather than a competitive, environment. This finding is consistent with that of other teachers using a similar approach.

Competition increases stress, which impedes learning. Physiologically, the stress of competition reduces the flow of blood to the small muscles, which, in turn, slows coordination.

Our talents expand naturally in a supportive environment. When tennis players begin their play by hitting the ball in a way that is easy for the other player to return, both develop a rhythm that leads to more consistent stroking. What is fascinating to observe is that each intuitively knows when the other player is able to return more challenging shots. Not only does the level of play improve rapidly, but the time the ball remains in play also increases substantially. It becomes clear to the participants that hitting the ball is more fun than retrieving balls that are not returned.

For those players who have extraordinary talent, the same approach will result in the greatest satisfaction. Following principle, each player hits his best shot as a way of supporting the talents and skills of the other player in making his best return. A player who is attached to a particular outcome, such as winning, diminishes the quality of his play. Attachment to anything retards progress. When both play the game for the joy and fun of it, they naturally raise the level of the game to the highest that each is capable of. This occurs as an outgrowth of their support of each other.

Not only is it inefficient to compete, it is also self-destructive. It is impossible for me to compete against you and try to beat you without beating myself. In withdrawing or withholding love from you, I withhold it from myself. Love is indivisible. I either share it with everyone, or I withhold it from myself.

The cause of pain is always the same. It is a withholding of love. Competition is painful. The elation of the victor is short-lived. Very soon the winner realizes how temporary his position is. Victory is always the prelude to a defense. It is a position of instability and uncertainty. It does not lead to peacefulness and joy.

The rewards given to the victor and withheld from the loser promote the misperception that it is necessary to compete to succeed. Success is a gift, along with life itself. We deprive ourselves of success when we believe that it is not already ours. It is impossible to win success. We feel success; we believe we are successful; and then we experience success. *Success comes from consciousness*.

There is another aspect of competition that deserves attention. What happens to a person who is physically or intellectually

108

unable to compete successfully? Whenever any person perceives that she is not good enough to compete or win, she is discouraged and loses the incentive to express who she is, fully and freely. Is life really only for those who seem to be able to win?

The costs to society from the belief that competition is helpful or useful are enormous. Everyone is talented and has something valuable to offer. Society benefits when each member is encouraged to believe that she is valuable, worthy, and can be all that she is capable of being.

A system based on competition assumes that only those who are willing and able to compete are worthy of the rewards of society. This seems to favor those who succeed at competitive endeavors. The truth is that it does not favor or benefit anyone. The discouragement and loss of incentive to contribute by those who see themselves as unable to compete is obvious. What is not so obvious is the extraordinary cost to those who try to win and who do win.

The cost is stress—the opposite of inner peace. Whatever the outward gain of competition, the inner loss is monumental. *It is the absence of inner peace that is the basis for the physical and emotional discomforts from which so many in our society suffer.*

Physical and emotional illness, requiring billions of dollars in medical, drug, and psychotherapeutic support leads to loss of time from employment and school. It also creates tension among family members.

Now consider how we benefit from mutual support. Not only do we avoid the dramatic costs of stress-related disorders, we gain the enormous benefits of encouraging each member of society to contribute all that she is capable of giving. The more we love and support each other, the richer, fuller, and more abundant our lives are.

# FREEDOM

What does freedom mean to the average person? It means the right to choose a career, a place to live, and a place to worship. It means the right to vote, to state our views in public, and to invest money as we wish. Our perception of freedom is being able to demand, and then protect, all the rights we feel entitled to enjoy.

What is freedom as a principle? It derives from our state of consciousness. *We experience freedom when we truly feel free within our being.*

Each individual feels a different amount of freedom. The variation is a result of different perceptions within. We imprison ourselves with our thoughts and beliefs. For example, there are people who live in neighborhoods they consider unsafe, and thus they rarely leave their apartments. There are many people who work long hours and commute long distances. They have very little free time and spend much of it recovering from exhaustion. Both groups are technically free, but in a functional sense, they are imprisoned.

There are many other misperceptions that result in freedom being more hypothetical than real.

Freedom is achieved when we feel free—free of attachment to the material world, free of judgments and expectations, free to express who we really are, and free to love everyone and everything unconditionally, just the way they are.

Freedom is a choice. It is a choice to give freedom to everything and everyone so that it may be reciprocated.

Accompanying freedom is responsibility. This is usually overlooked by the person demanding freedom. The person demanding freedom to speak his mind has the responsibility to allow others to speak freely. The person demanding the right to vote has the responsibility to allow the same freedom for everyone. If we wish the freedom to use a public park, we are responsible for caring for it and keeping it clean for others who wish to use it.

The reason that so few people recognize the balancing factor of responsibility when they demand freedom is that they have placed freedom outside of themselves. Whatever is outside of us is experienced as temporary, uncertain, and subject to forces beyond our control. We fought for the freedoms granted in our Constitution and still believe that we must fight to keep them.

Freedom is never outside of us; it is always within. Having it within guarantees that it will be experienced. To free ourselves in consciousness is a choice and then a commitment.

When we recognize that we are One in truth, we shall gladly support another's freedom. When we love ourselves unconditionally, we shall feel the same about each other and, thus, everyone's freedom is assured.

# MARRIAGE

Marriage is a contractual relationship, combined with an oath. It is probably one of the most solemn ceremonies people choose to celebrate. In spite of the solemnity, oaths, and written agreements, approximately 50 percent of marriages end in divorce. Obviously the average couple does not understand what is involved in a marital relationship.

It is clear that written agreements are of no practical consequence, regardless of how many witnesses there are or how solemn the original intention was. When one or both of the parties is finished with the relationship, it ends.

Since the contract, the ceremony, and the oath are unable to bind the parties to one another, what are the factors that do?

In order for any relationship to be successful, it must be voluntary. A successful marriage is one which honors the principle of free will and free choice. In a successful marriage, the parties continually recommit themselves to each other and to the marriage. They also surrender to a purpose larger than themselves. Out of the surrender to a higher purpose comes a willingness to surrender to each other.

In essence, a successful marriage is one in which the parties desire to experience unconditional love. Since love is indivisible, it is felt and expressed, not only for the spouse, but also for all with whom there is contact. Every experience with the spouse is an opportunity to deepen the feeling of unconditional love and then share it with others. Every experience with others is an opportunity to deepen the feeling of unconditional love that can then be brought back to the marriage.

A successful marriage requires each participant to have a strong sense of self. Many people entering a marriage believe that

113

it is a joining of two people, each of whom is incomplete in some way and who, by uniting, will complete each other. This is impossible. To be successful, a marriage joins two individuals, each of whom is whole and complete. Any need that the partner must fill is a demand that cannot be met. *Principle is clear that no one can fill a void in another.* Any such attempt is doomed to fail. *Each person must master his own life. He cannot waive this requirement by having another offer to do it for him.*

The role we can choose to play in each other's lives is to be unconditionally loving and supportive, so that those in our presence feel encouraged to tell the truth to themselves. This supports them in gaining the insights needed to correct any misperceptions they have about themselves and others.

By joining in marriage, what we hope to do is pledge unconditional love and support to each other under all of the many circumstances and challenges that we create. It is an opportunity to feel unconditional love deeply and consistently. It is a way of supporting each other in staying on the cutting edge of life and gaining the most joy possible from the experience. As the love and support for each other grow, they are reflected back in more and more loving experiences. Life becomes an ever-expanding circle of love.

# OWNERSHIP

The American dream is ownership: to own our own homes, cars, boats, and stocks. The general perception is that the more we own, the more successful and secure we become. Ownership is based on the assumption that life is a very personal, individual experience of self-aggrandizement; that the resources of the world belong to anyone who is capable of appropriating them, limited only by the rules of society. These rules agree with the basic assumption that owning more is better. They just attempt to make the distribution more orderly.

There is also an assumption that some resources are best kept for community use. Thus the various governments allocate land for parks and other general use. Such allocations constitute a very small percentage of the whole and do not significantly impede the flow of resources to private ownership.

What does principle have to say about this? Anyone who truly believes that abundance is the natural state of affairs in the Universe has no attachment to the concept of ownership as it is customarily understood. From the viewpoint of principle, an owner is a caretaker.

As with life itself, everything is a gift to everyone. It is here for us to share. It is also here for us to appreciate and to respect. Anyone who is grateful for a gift naturally cares for it. Anyone who believes the supply of gifts is infinite naturally shares them generously.

There is a practical problem facing those who believe in limitation and appropriation rather than abundance. They keep acting out their own belief systems. In their attachment to what they have, they block the natural flow of abundance.

Appropriators believe that they must hoard while they are strong enough to do so, because when they become older or weaker they will need to draw upon the hoard. Yet the stress of attempting to appropriate and accumulate—contrary to the natural order—creates illness and aging.

It is helpful to ask ourselves which is more important: cars, houses, stocks, and bonds or loving, supportive people in our lives? Since both alternatives are available to us, it is interesting to note that we favor the accumulation of possessions. In fact, we regularly sacrifice love and support in order to accumulate things, though we know in our hearts that love is more satisfying.

The guidelines of our society encourage us to strive to accumulate more and more, telling us that we will always have time to enjoy the love and support of others. Somehow, this does not happen. The inability to relate successfully to one another is the hallmark of our world. This is true from simple one-to-one relationships to relationships among sovereign governments.

There is a solution. Principle tells us that means and ends are identical. Whatever means we choose to achieve a particular result is the result.

Choosing self-denial, struggle, and an adversarial approach to life, as a way of ultimately achieving a life of ease and tranquillity, does not work. All we accomplish is mastering self-denial, struggle, and aggressiveness. Ease and tranquillity remain a foreign experience. Having never practiced it, we do not even know what it is. Achieving a life of ease and tranquillity means living life moment by moment and day by day in an easy and tranquil manner.

The solution is simple. Caretakers, whose experience is that abundance is the natural state of affairs, disarm those who believe they have to appropriate, accumulate, and be aggressive. This leads to a redefinition of ownership as a voluntary assumption of responsibility to care for and share the abundance of the Universe in a spirit of gratitude and appreciation.

# SUPERSTARS

Ours is a society that creates and honors superstars. This practice is encouraged by the entertainment industry, of which sports is a major segment. It has spread to many other parts of society, such as business, finance, the professions, and the arts.

Not only does society allocate vast sums to support this system, there is a much larger cost that seems to go unnoticed.

The assumption underlying the superstar system, as we presently practice it, is that there are a limited number of superstar positions available. The corollary to this is that most people cannot be superstars. This is a direct contradiction of principle. It undermines the fact that each of us is a unique, talented, and exquisite entity in a Universe that supports and encourages full participation by each of its essential elements.

As with any masterpiece, all of the components are an equally valuable part of the whole. Can we remove one color from a painting? Can we eliminate a part of a sculpture or a section of a play? Every voice in a choir, instrument in an orchestra, supporting actor in a drama, and mechanic in a factory is important.

Society's superstar approach discourages most of us from believing we are superstars. Life is a totally subjective experience. We create our own importance by believing it.

Life would be more fun for everyone if we treated each other as superstars. It would encourage all of us to fully and freely express ourselves, allowing our talents and unique qualities to lovingly support those with whom we come in contact.

Let us look at this from the viewpoint of the principle of abundance. Once we agree that there is enough for everyone, and we are willing to share generously with each other, it becomes obvious that the more we share, the more abundant we feel. There is no limit. The ability to be generous is infinite. We also learn that the material world contains the least significant aspects of abundance.

To enjoy each other's unique qualities and talents, we must learn to support each other lovingly in expressing who we really are. In our rush to value certain skills and talents more than others, we encourage many to discard their natural talents and to develop skills that bring more money and status.

To experience the limitlessness of abundance, we must learn to appreciate the equality of all talents, unique qualities, and ways of expression. We do not have to enjoy them all equally, or choose to experience them, but all of us benefit when we give everyone the unconditional love and support to fully and freely express who she is, as an equal.

Life is similar to a large symphony orchestra. Each instrument is of equal importance. We can enjoy the unique sound of our own instrument even more when we join with others to make rich, beautiful, and harmonious music.

# ADVERSITY

Illness, loss of a job, or a robbery are only a few of the many adversities that seem to be a constant in our daily lives. When we experience adversity, it invariably arouses emotions such as sadness, anger, or frustration.

In terms of principle, adversity is a mirroring of what we believe. The fascinating part of this is that as each of us experiences the same or similar events, we respond differently to them.

It is generally agreed that war, with its pain, suffering, and killing, is one of the most adverse circumstances in life. Yet each front-line soldier responds in a way that is unique to him. One soldier may feel inspired by the opportunity to defend his country, a second may feel uneasy about shooting at the enemy, and a third may desert because of his unwillingness to shoot at anyone.

The same applies to adversities of a relatively minor nature. Each person who cuts his finger responds differently. Some hardly notice; others run for medical assistance; still others use it as an excuse not to wash the dishes.

It is important to know that regardless of our prior response, we have the opportunity to change our reaction at any time.

Free choice and our willingness to recognize that nothing outside of us need cause us pain are the operative principles. The pain is always self-created and results from our unwillingness to love ourselves just the way we are.

While many of the events that come into our lives are a result of a group consciousness, and thus are not under our individual control, our response is always under our own control. Seeing anyone and any event as less than perfect proves that we are being judgmental. Judging anything is a withholding of love. The result is fear, followed by pain.

The knowing part of each of us is always creating the precise circumstances we require to enable us to release judgment, see only perfection,* express only love, and feel only joy.

# ADVICE

"A lawyer's advice is his stock in trade." This statement, attributed to Abraham Lincoln, has adorned the wall of many an attorney's office. Other professionals have adopted the idea. We now buy advice from financial consultants, management consultants, educational consultants, and even spiritual consultants.

Ours is called the Information Age, and one of its major businesses is selling information. Much of this information comes in the form of advice. When we do not buy advice from professionals, we seek it from friends, relatives, and acquaintances. In our society, we act as though everyone knows more than we do. Though we may not realize it, acting this way undermines our self-confidence and self-esteem.

Principle tells us that we are born knowing everything. We believe, however, that we know very little and learn what we need to know from books and from experience. Though young children continually mirror the truth to us, we often insist that they are not only wrong but also misbehaving. Sometimes we even punish them.

We can recall knowingness when we are willing to release the belief that we know very little. Knowingness is a feeling. It is felt as intuition. Something either feels true or it doesn't.

One person's truth may be different at any given time from another person's truth. This results from the evolutionary nature of our being. We are each at a different stage of development, a different stage of consciousness. This does not mean that one is right and the other is wrong. It just means that the same event or circumstance seems different at various stages. When we become aware of our knowingness, we recognize that we have always had it and so has everyone else.

As individuals and in groups, the way we support each other in our growth is by loving each other just the way we are. Conversely, the way we discourage each other from growth is by judging. This is especially true for children. Infants and young children are close to their knowingness. With continued support in freely expressing it—which is another way of saying, expressing who they really are just the way they are—they can easily blend their truth with society's reality.

Society's reality has no power over a person's knowingness. Inner knowing contains the power of the Universe, and it is a totally benign power. It is a power that brings inner peace and tranquillity, a sense of safety, so that everyone is perceived as friendly.

Thus, I would like to modify Lincoln's statement slightly. I suggest that it read, "A person's advice to himself, felt from within, is his own stock in trade." He needs no other.

# DETAILS

We make lists for shopping, appointments, and chores. To these we add details related to careers or businesses. We often purchase books and take courses to assist us in more efficiently handling details in our lives.

We place something on a list when we perceive it as an obligation. We tend to remember those things we enjoy. Appointments with the doctor or the dentist are marked on our calendars. We easily remember the dates of our vacations.

The principle that applies is very simple. *Every detail that creates any discomfort is a way we have chosen to block the feeling of joyfulness.*

Doctors, dentists, employers, spouses, and friends can be a source of fun and support. They can also be a source of anxiety and frustration. When the experience is the latter, it becomes a detail we have to handle. The choice is always ours.

As we look around, we find some people whose lives are easy and simple. They choose careers that are outlets for their talents, spend time with friends they love, and express their creativity in ways they enjoy. In contrast are those whose lives are often uncomfortable. Their choices reflect a chaotic consciousness.

Allowing ourselves to experience joyfulness most of the time requires a great deal of commitment to principle. A person who has established a pattern of struggle or suffering must recognize that the existing pattern is, by definition, supported by 100 percent intention. He will not succeed in releasing it until the intention to change reaches the same level.

Our basic feeling state is joyfulness. Peeling off the many layers of beliefs and patterns that block our connection to it is a major undertaking.

Adopting an alternative belief system to universal principles is the main way we bring into being the details that block our natural state of joyfulness. Some examples are:

We work at a job that we do not enjoy to make money to "earn a living" and find ourselves performing many tasks and handling many details that we dislike.

We hold on to resentments and angers toward our parents, refuse to feel forgiveness, and then do things for them that we find annoying out of a sense of obligation.

We believe we have worked too hard to pay the government as much in taxes as it demands and feel resistant to filing tax returns and paying taxes.

On the other hand, when we use universal principles as our guidelines and define and follow our purpose, *our lives become much simpler.* We notice that there are fewer details to handle. Feeling that our lives are purposeful and meaningful, we notice that tasks that we previously performed out of a sense of obligation are now ways to show support and love for others.

When we open to the love and support of the Universe, we realize we are eager to have our lives be fun and full of joy. It is then that we allow ourselves to enter careers that are an expression of our talents and we do what we love to do. It is also then that we allow ourselves to experience relationships that are nurturing, loving, and supportive.

Many of the details that we handle on a daily basis, such as shopping and washing the dishes, can be fun or annoying. The major factor in determining the way we experience these tasks is how much we are enjoying the other parts of our day. If we are doing what we love, are free of stress, have time to be with friends, take vacations, and in other ways feel fulfilled, the normal, daily details become fun also. If our jobs and relationships are stressful and frustrating and allow us little free time to spend with friends and take vacations, the simple details such as shopping and washing the dishes seem like burdens.

Finally, those of us who are doing what we love are handling details for each other, not as details, but as something we enjoy.

The Universe, in Its infinite wisdom, has given us such a broad range of talents that when each of us expresses these talents, all the details of our lives are handled easily and in an enjoyable way. Life becomes a simple expression of Oneness, with each of us adding to the joyfulness of each other's life, while simultaneously adding to the joyfulness of our own.

# SEX

Sexual energy is a part of the human condition. It is sufficiently strong and reliable that it is used as the motivating force for much that occurs in our society. Advertisers, clothing designers, movie-makers, and authors use it to gain our attention.

To understand sexual energy requires an understanding of the relationship between our Essence and our body. Our body mirrors the state of our consciousness. The body is a magnificent vehicle that tells us the truth about ourselves. In our society, the story it relates is how we distort who we really are.

Principle tells us that there is only one basic, underlying feeling—joyfulness. When we love unconditionally, with our hearts wide open, we feel joyfulness. It is the natural setting for us to play together.

Joyfulness does not require physical expression to enhance it. Joyfulness is the feeling of our connection with our Source. It is an honoring of who we really are and who everyone else really is. It is an ecstatic state and cannot be improved upon.

The act of sex, as we commonly interpret it, is a physical experience. The participants stimulate each other visually and through touch. These stimuli often replace the basic feeling of joyfulness, grounded in unconditional love.

This is not to say that sex is always a distortion of unconditional love. It can be an extension of unconditional love for those of us who allow ourselves a relationship of this kind with our sexual partners. When the emphasis is on the physical aspects of the relationship, the partner is often treated as a sexual object.

To be at peace with our sexuality, it is helpful to understand the simple prerequisites to truly satisfying and mutually supportive relationships.

127

First, we must be committed to the relationship. Commitment means 100 percent intention to support the relationship, regardless of its duration. It can be a casual one that lasts only a minute or a long-term one such as marriage.

Commitment is a concept that is basic to our achieving anything in our lives. It is impossible to accomplish something without first reaching a 100 percent intention to have it. This is another way of defining commitment.

The Universe provides us with a very simple mathematical system that governs our personal affairs. This system only registers or notices zero and 100 percent. Until our intention to have something, or achieve a change in our beliefs reaches 100 percent, the sought-after result does not occur.

There is another way of looking at commitment. It is the level of intention required to be a fully *aware* player in the game of life. Our Souls mandate that we play in the game of life. They forever move us along, but it is our choice whether or not to align with our Souls. We do this through awareness. This literally means being awake as we go through life. It means *feeling our feelings as we respond to the experiences that our Souls create.*

Commitment can only be in the moment. In a long-term relationship, the parties continually recommit themselves. Sustaining the commitment for many years is no guarantee that either or both participants will continue it in the next moment.

Once we are ready to proceed at the commitment level, there are three relationships that we must master. First, we must do what it takes to make peace with and feel unconditional love for the Universe, our home. We deepen this primary relationship, our connection to the Intelligence that created us, and we are grateful for the love and support that It provides for us moment by moment. We are aware of our trust in this love and support and know that we are safe and secure wherever we are. We feel the abundance of the Universe and are eager to share it with others. This becomes our commitment to the Universe.

The second relationship is with ourselves. This means making peace with and feeling unconditional love for ourselves. We do what we have to do to truly accept ourselves just the way we are;

we feel good about ourselves just the way we are; and we love ourselves just the way we are. We gain the feeling of commitment to ourselves.

The final relationship is the one we have with others. This means sharing with everyone the love we have for the Universe and for ourselves. We know we have accomplished this when our relationships with family, friends, and acquaintances are peaceful and mutually supportive. When we feel our commitment, we are ready to open ourselves to an exclusive relationship, if that is our desire.

An exclusive relationship is not more loving than any other. It is one in which we give ourselves the opportunity to express unconditional love and support for another person, under all of the varying circumstances that life offers. It tests our patience, our perseverance, and our willingness to keep our hearts open consistently. It also allows us to expand our expressions of love and deepen our feelings of joyfulness.

An exclusive relationship is one in which we agree to share certain intimacies with only one partner. However, the heart-opening experiences we have with our partners enable us to relate to others with more love and more compassion. A successful, exclusive relationship is one that matures through a series of steps: first, respect; then friendship; next, intimacy; and finally, surrender.

Respect is treating another person in the same way that we wish to be treated. It is a demonstration that we value the other person.

Friendship is the stage of getting to know another person and naturally feeling comfortable with him or her. It usually takes time. The more experiences we have with a friend, the greater the certainty that there is a true bond of friendship. We call a person a friend when we feel love for the person consistently, regardless of the circumstances that occur. Friendship occurs when we know enough about the patterns and attitudes of the person that there are no big surprises in the relationship.

Intimacy occurs when friendship reaches total trust. It is a sharing of deeply personal thoughts and feelings, and a readiness to surrender to the partner. This demonstrates total trust and confidence in the unconditional love and support of the partner under all circumstances. While time is not an issue, it usually takes time for the relationship to progress through all of these stages of friendship, respect, intimacy, and surrender.

To insure a fulfilling and completely satisfying experience, the physical act of sex best occurs after the prior steps of respect, friendship, intimacy, and surrender are completed. It is then more than a physical experience; it is a bonding of Essences.

We often use sex in an attempt to release anxieties and frustrations, the way we use alcohol and drugs. When our lives are not loving and peaceful, having sex is not a loving and supportive experience. We bring the withholding of love and the unwillingness to forgive directly into our relationships with our sexual partners.

The energies of the Universe are powerful. It is not self-supportive to think that we can quickly and easily release all the beliefs we have practiced and honored for many years. Until we do, however, sexual energy cannot be a totally positive force.

We do not give a power saw to a child. We should not allow ourselves to play at sex without first truly appreciating what we are dealing with. It is an act of self-love to be honest about the degree of mastery we have attained in living our lives according to universal principles.

Taking the simple steps outlined above allows the powerful energies of the Universe to flow freely through us, leaving us joyful, grateful, and humble. It is in this spirit that the act of sex becomes the way we express unconditional love and support for our partners, ourselves, and the Universe.

# PROFESSIONALS

Professionals are a privileged group in our society. After years of training and experience, they are permitted to offer specialized services to members of the community in exchange for a promise to abide by standards of behavior that are more exacting than those required of a person not classified as a professional.

When society confers special privileges upon the professional, it also creates the opportunity for a perception of inequality between the professional and the patient or client. This has happened to a large extent in our society. The public is encouraged to turn over its responsibility for its health care to doctors and its responsibility for deciding when and how to make claims and defend itself from the claims of others to lawyers.

Since the professional is given the authority to make these decisions, and since he is rewarded financially for making them, it is not surprising that many individuals have turned their power over to the professionals.

In undertaking this responsibility, however, the professional has opened himself to the liability that arises when the results from the decision seem unsatisfactory to the patient or client. We see the consequences in the mounting claims for malpractice against doctors and lawyers.

The effects of giving away power are much greater than the professional, the patient, or the client realizes. While at first look it appears easier to allow the professional to make the decisions, no one really feels comfortable when he is in a position of inequality and powerlessness. This is true even when the result is favorable.

It also explains why we are so harsh in our judgment of the professional when the result is unsatisfactory. If we felt grateful for

131

the willingness of the professional to undertake the responsibility, we would be less eager to claim malpractice.

Before the age of specialization, and when the professional was more a friend of the family, malpractice suits were rare. During this period of time, the patient or the client did not feel unequal and powerless. He felt cared for, nurtured, and grateful. If the result achieved was less than successful, the patient or client accepted the responsibility along with the professional.

The movement toward increasing specialization in both medicine and law has created less personalized care and a greater sense of alienation. This has intensified the perception of inequality and powerlessness.

The solution is simple. *Principle tells us that we are all equal and we are all equally powerful.* Having professionals with specialized training is fine, provided the services they deliver are offered in a caring, nurturing way that acknowledges the inherent equality of the parties.

Under the principle of giving and receiving, the primary reward of anyone is the gift he gives himself when he serves another. The more loving the service, the greater the benefit to the giver. Financial reward can never replace the deep satisfaction, sense of fulfillment, and joyfulness of serving another with love.

When a patient or client is served lovingly, he is not only grateful, he also feels empowered. He is eager to take responsibility and be a co-partner in the entire experience, including the result.

# ARCHITECTS AND ENGINEERS

The role of the architect in our society is to design structures. When she is successful, she creates a perfect synthesis of form and function. The balance between confined and open space inspires both the viewer and the user.

The role of the engineer is to design and evaluate systems and products. When she is successful, she simplifies our lives and adds to the pleasure of our day.

We ensure that these structures, products, and systems are consistently of the highest quality by clearly defining the role and purpose in the community of the professionals who design and evaluate them.

The purpose of architects and engineers is to express their talents in support of their local communities and the larger community of which we are all a part. Ideally, before a structure, system, or product is designed, the professionals ask themselves, "Are we serving the user, the community, the environment, and all of humankind with our creations? Will we improve the quality of life for all?"

Do we love ourselves enough to ask these questions?

# DOCTORS

I use the term *doctor* to include physicians, chiropractors, dentists, and other practitioners who are authorized by the community to offer curative services. We call upon them when an uncomfortable physical condition appears beyond our ability to control it. When we feel a degree of pain that is unacceptable, we expect a doctor to relieve it.

The body is dependent upon consciousness for its support. It is, however, a vehicle that can assist us in correcting our misperceptions. Painful conditions alert us to the choices we have made that are unloving to ourselves. When we heed the body's signals, we are given ample opportunity to change our perception and clear our consciousness. In this way we avert symptoms.

The role of a doctor can be as a master of healing. He can teach us to be so sensitive to our body's signals that we can release misperceptions simply, easily, and before we experience any significant discomfort. A true healer teaches and demonstrates how all pain is a withholding of love from ourselves and often from another.

We can support ourselves and doctors during the transition from the traditional method of doctoring to the practice of self-healing by following these suggestions:

*First,* it is important to honor our present beliefs. If we feel comfortable having the support of a traditional doctor, we continue with the use of that support. It is not helpful to make believe that our beliefs are different than they are.

*Second,* we take more responsibility for our own health care. We ask questions to understand the treatment program and how we can assist in the process.

135

*Third,* we feel love for the doctor and for ourselves. This will free him to mirror back to us our love and support for him.

*Fourth,* we focus on principle, using It as the basis for our lives. This is the way to true healing.

The state of the art of doctoring always reflects the state of consciousness of the community. The particular doctor each of us chooses reflects the state of our own consciousness. In order to become self-healers, we must first be at peace with ourselves just the way we are.

The symptoms we have are perfect. The knowing part of us created them. Healing occurs when we use the symptoms to guide us to release the misperceptions that gave rise to them. We are all capable of self-healing when we are ready.

# LAWYERS

Lawyers draft agreements, prepare wills, and act as our representatives in making claims and defending us against claims made by others. They write laws and then they interpret the laws they have written. As society has grown more complex, so have the agreements, wills, lawsuits, and laws.

Let us examine the role these services play in our lives. When a friend borrows money or a car or a lawn mower, we do not first engage a lawyer to prepare a loan agreement. We trust that our friend will return what he has borrowed in a timely manner and in good condition.

*Life is simple when there is trust and friendship.*

As our society has grown more impersonal, very few of the people we interact with are considered friends. We choose written agreements to replace the trust relationship we have with friends.

There must be something bothersome in this arrangement. No one can feel truly at peace with the substitution of a document for a personal relationship. What is uncomfortable is that beneath all the complexity and sophistication of our society there remains an unacknowledged need of everyone to relate in a loving manner. Whenever this deep need is unrecognized, the substitute arrangement develops flaws and causes discomfort.

The discomfort we feel with abiding by all the laws in our society has nothing to do with the laws. It has to do with placing our focus on a system that attempts to replace something that is real with a fiction.

Each person's experience with the law reflects her own state of consciousness. People who are at peace within themselves have no difficulty living in a society based on adversarial law.

137

As society moves in the direction of less competition and more mutual support, the role of the lawyer changes correspondingly. He becomes the teacher and practitioner of universal law. Just as doctors can support patients in healing themselves, lawyers can support clients in being their own universal lawyers.

Universal law is natural to all of us. It provides the framework and support for us to recognize who we really are and how we are connected to one another. It is perfectly natural for all of us to be our own universal lawyers.

# UNCERTAINTY

A reasonable description of the underlying attitude of the average person leaving home in the morning is uncertainty. It is supported, even encouraged, by television and newspaper reports of accidents, rapidly changing economic and business conditions, wars, and unstable political environments worldwide.

We have adapted to uncertainty in a number of ways. Many of us assume that there is little or nothing that we can do to alter a situation. However, that assumption does not satisfy our underlying need for certainty. The result is continual discomfort, which expresses itself, according to the mirror principle, in the re-creation of experiences of uncertainty.

Another response to uncertainty is an attempt to limit the effects of the circumstances we fear. We purchase insurance, put money into savings, obtain extensive credentials, and achieve the apparent protection of seniority in our jobs.

Since these approaches are not in alignment with principle, the result is an escalation in discomfort, which the Universe mandates as a way of encouraging us to view the situation differently. If we fail to read the signal and change our perception, we experience even more discomfort and uneasiness.

What is the true solution to this frustrating and ever more painful experience? Principle tells us that life is inherently an experience of certainty. The Universe, always being on purpose, is the epitome of stability and constancy. Whenever we open to Its love and support, we feel it.

Moving from the belief in uncertainty, our starting place, to the belief in certainty can be compared to the experience of a sailor bringing a ship to shore. As long as the sailor focuses on the guideposts that are known to be invariable, he can direct the ship with confidence. The guideposts can be stars, a lighthouse, or radar. In the case of the Universe, the guideposts are universal principles.

Inner peace, harmony, abundance, and joyfulness are basic to the human condition, but we must reaffirm them until they become our dominant beliefs. This process pushes against our existing beliefs that we are not deserving, not capable, not lovable, and not trustworthy.

Regardless of prior experience, it is possible for all of us to align with universal principles. This means bringing our purpose into awareness, feeling it, and then feeling the peacefulness, harmony, abundance, and joyfulness that grow out of it.

It is for each person to decide the importance of enjoying the certainty of inner peace in any situation. While it seems simple when thought about in an abstract way, it becomes challenging when the alternative to inner peace is appealing. In the presence of someone who tests our patience, we can easily choose a caustic remark instead of one that is loving and supportive. Feeling anxious about taking an examination that is important to our career advancement, we can easily fall back on old patterns of test taking that are not efficient, rather than allow time to relax and feel confident.

Inner peace is that centered, balanced, grounded place that frees us to be aware of what is going on without judgment. It is a state of being that inspires creativity and encourages us to be supportive of ourselves and others. It is our natural state.

When we choose a feeling other than inner peace, it is helpful to be aware that we have done so. What is not helpful is selecting other than inner peace without any awareness that a choice has been made.

This leads to the question of how we know when any choice we have made is the perfect one for us. The answer is simple. When we have chosen the perfect alternative, we feel at peace with the choice. When we experience any discomfort, we know it is best to choose again. If we continue to choose until we are at peace, we reach the perfect choice.

Finally, the distractions of our daily lives, coupled with our existing belief systems that are contrary to principle, mandate that we seek the support of like-intentioned friends.

When people join in support of one another, there is usually at least one in the group who is capable of inspiring those who are discouraged to continue.

The Universe is a model mutual support system. The support group, as a mirror of that model, is a perfect vehicle to a life based on principle, filled with certainty and inner peace.

# GUILT

It is truly amazing how much of our behavior is motivated by guilt. Every time we act out of guilt, we reinforce the feeling in our consciousness.

Guilt and obligation go hand in hand. Feeling guilty, we discipline ourselves to act out of a sense of obligation. For example, because we feel guilty about not visiting our parents, we force ourselves to make periodic visits. Feeling guilty about having more than the poor and the disabled have, we give to charity. The list is endless. Acting out of obligation demonstrates our true desire to connect with one another, no matter what the cost.

Principle tells us that guilt is a cousin to fear. The underlying dynamics are the same. Fear and guilt are both symptoms that result from a withholding of love. In the case of guilt, we withhold love from ourselves because we judge ourselves as bad or unworthy. For all the myriad ways that guilt expresses itself in our lives there is only one solution: We must refrain from withholding love from ourselves.

In the quiet of your own room, when you are feeling relatively peaceful, bring the person or situation about which you feel guilty into consciousness and feel forgiveness for yourself. Practice this daily, until the feeling of forgiveness releases love. Continue the process until you feel only love. You can accelerate the process by standing in front of a mirror, looking yourself in the eyes, and stating your name, smiling, and then saying, "I love you and accept you just the way you are." Repeat this a few times a day, for a minute each time.

As the feeling of guilt recedes and love for ourselves grows, visits to our parents and gifts to charity take on a different quality.

The feeling of obligation is replaced with the joy of sharing and expressing our love.

How we see ourselves is how we see others. Learning to feel love for ourselves enables us to feel love for others. This leaves no room for guilt.

# ADDICTIONS AND PATTERNS

The average person looks upon an addict as a breed apart. Society defines an addict as a kind of emotional cripple—a person whose relationship to his habit is close to helplessness. What is overlooked in this appraisal is that some of the habit patterns that each of us has are closer to addictions than we realize.

*Addiction is a pattern that is adopted to keep us out of the present.* When we really focus in the present, we open to it at a feeling level. This puts us in touch with ourselves and all that is around us. In order to be fully in the present, we must open our hearts. Since we cannot feel selectively, the opening process exposes our tender areas, the places in us that have been sensitized by experiences that we still perceive as nonloving and nonsupportive. These include all the inadequacies and rejections that are alive within us, all the angers, anxieties, and desire for retribution that we have stored.

It seems to the rest of us that the energy devoted by the addict to avoidance of opening to these feelings is extreme and unrealistic. Yet every pattern serves the same purpose of keeping us out of the present.

Being totally in the present and feeling all that we experience as we go through our day is something that none of us has learned to do. In fact, to a large extent we have mastered the opposite— closing down, at a feeling level, to most of our experiences. An addict is mirroring for us, in a rather extreme way, how we approach our lives.

The conclusions we have reached about the challenges facing an addict in releasing his habit pattern applies to everyone.

145

Releasing a pattern does require 100 percent intention and a constant recommitment to releasing it in every present moment. For those of us whose patterns have not reached the status of an addiction, either by our own or by society's standard, the remainder of the chapter can be read to gain insight about any pattern and how to release it.

The perception of those of us with addictive patterns is that we are not acceptable the way we are. We believe that something is wrong with us. We have attempted to fix it by acting in ways that bring approval and acceptance, yet this only intensifies our belief that being who we are, just the way we are, is not acceptable. Finally, we give up trying to fix what is wrong, concluding that it is beyond fixing.

The more painful our sense of what is buried, the more determined we are to avoid uncovering it and feeling it. Alcohol, drugs, gambling, and overeating are patterns that serve us well in desensitizing ourselves to this pain. These kinds of patterns numb us and seem to move us further from the pain, but they really remove us further from the present. The more we depart from the present, the greater the pain. In reality, the pain is caused by feeling our separation from our Source, which we replay by separating ourselves from family and friends.

The strong emotional component of the addictive pattern anchors it deeply within our consciousness. At first the pattern is more important and meaningful to the addict than he realizes. When an addict finally acknowledges an addiction, he treats it with great respect. He recognizes the feeling of powerlessness he experiences when dealing with it.

It is helpful to understand that we have many patterns that make us feel powerless but that we fail to recognize as addictions. For example, there are many people who have addictive patterns about money. Some continually create more debt than income. These people are plagued by an irresistible urge to spend. Others are addicted to work; they are the so-called workaholics.

There are people who have addictive patterns with relationships. Many of them attract relationships that are uncommitted and unfulfilling. They are people who are looking for love outside of themselves. There are people who are addicted to finding faults in others. They resist feeling forgiveness for anyone.

How, then, does a person rid himself of an addiction? First he creates the context for change—the awareness of his connection to the Universe and the feeling of Its love and support. He realizes that the Universe is on his side, not against him. Defining his purpose in universal terms and reading it often is a perfect way to begin. Maintaining the feeling of love and support from the Universe in consciousness is absolutely essential.

Next he recognizes that the addiction has been created consciously and can be released consciously. The operative principle is free will. Though an addict has sometimes forgotten when and how he adopted the addictive pattern, he made a conscious choice at some earlier time. All behavior is a conscious choice, even though most of us prefer not to see it that way.

When he recognizes that he chose the addiction, the addict is ready to acknowledge the existence of all of his judgments relating to the addiction. These include his judgment of those who he believes failed to love him unconditionally, as well as his judgment of himself for not being worthy of any love.

Releasing judgments is a major undertaking. I suggest selecting one person with whom your relationship is less than satisfying. Every day, in the quiet of your room, bring this person into consciousness. Feel the presence of this person. Then feel forgiveness for him. It is most important that this not be done in an intellectual way. Stay with the feeling, whatever it may be.

The feeling we have toward this person is the truth for us in the present moment. It is only by honoring this feeling and experiencing it fully that we can come to peace with the person whose behavior gave rise to it. We do this by opening our hearts to the feeling and to the person. Our hearts wash out the judgment that is attached to the feeling.

An essential part of releasing judgment is the recognition that we cannot do it alone. We must be willing to open to the support of the Universe and believe It is on our side, not our opponent.

147

We must remind ourselves of this constantly. What we are trying to accomplish each time is a little more willingness to open to however we feel.

Once we have a sense of progress with this part, we are ready to feel forgiveness for ourselves. Remember, every relationship we have mirrors our consciousness. If we are judging another, he really reflects a part of us of which we are critical. Feeling forgiveness for ourselves completes the cycle.

Feeling forgiveness for a key person in our lives is often a long-term project. It is best to eliminate time as an issue and just do the exercises every day. We reach a point when we notice the appearance of some feelings of love for the person. Continue with the exercise until just the thought of the person arouses only loving feelings.

The commitment to the process of releasing judgment, the awareness that we have a choice, and the recognition that the Universe is on our side prepares those of us who have addictions to marshal 100 percent intention to release our addictive patterns. Until we reach this level of commitment to ourselves, real change is impossible. When we reach it, we then create a structure, a self-disciplined procedure that we follow with total devotion. It becomes a daily routine of rebuilding our sense of self, a commitment to replace self-destructive behavior with actions that are self-supportive.

A word about structure and how it differs from a pattern. I define a structure as a series of actions that we create with total awareness of their purpose. Awareness is the key. In creating a structure, we are *consciously* performing acts that we believe are self-supportive and will help us to achieve a result that we desire.

A pattern is a repetition of actions that we allow to drop out of awareness. This is the opposite of what we are seeking to accomplish.

Another choice that may be part of an addict's structure, in addition to daily exercises of forgiveness, is facing himself in a mirror, smiling, and saying his name, followed by, "I love and accept you just the way you are." Yet another choice is to join a support group in which he can feel love and acceptance for being who he is just the way he is.

A person in the process of releasing an addictive pattern can monitor his progress by noticing the support he receives from others. Since we reflect the state of consciousness of each other, all improvement in our sense of self and our willingness to support ourselves will generate support from others.

A person's success in any endeavor is always a function of his openness to receive support. Successful people naturally marshal support. An addictive pattern is a clear statement of rejection of support. To reverse the process of rejection, a person needs to have this insight: *Anyone who rejects me is simply responding to my rejection of myself.*

I cannot overemphasize the importance of opening ourselves to support. As a mutual support system, the Universe is set up to provide all of the support we require to live a joyful, peaceful and abundant life, but until we open to the support, it might as well not be there.

The choice to keep an addiction alive is a choice to reject support. Remember, support requires us to open to it, at the *feeling* level. It is a heart-opening experience. While it is the door to joyfulness, for the addict it is perceived as the door to pain.

A word about chemical-dependency addictions. It is essential that an addict create a structure, or seek the support of an existing structure (treatment program), for the release of the physical dependency. It is also essential that the addict persevere until the physical aspects of the dependency are released. It is important to remember, however, that our consciousness controls our bodies. The greater our commitment to principle, the easier the detoxification process will be.

Most people believe that the detoxification process involves extreme pain. Therefore I wish to restate the definition of pain, so that it can be seen in this context. *Pain is the experience of fear in the physical body. Fear is always a withholding of love from ourselves, and often from another.* This means that pain is always a choice. It can be released when the person feeling it is willing to change his interpretation of the situation and feel love where it was previously withheld.

Since our preconceived ideas about ourselves, others and the life experience are so deeply held, changing them requires great commitment and perseverance. It is not more difficult to release pain in one situation than in another. The so-called degrees of pain we feel are totally subjective.

The brain is the organ that controls all physical processes. Remember, however, that our consciousness controls our brains. We feel pain when we wish to. It is always a choice. The choice can be the result of one or more of an infinite number of reasons. *No one can know why another person makes any choice about an aspect of his personal life.*

We complicate and confuse the situation by our adoption of commonly held beliefs. Therefore it is assumed that certain situations result in pain. Yet not everyone experiences pain in all of these situations, much less the same degree of pain.

Let me give an example. We are all familiar with the fact that having a tooth drilled is a vastly different experience for each dental patient. Some people require anesthesia; others require none. Having stated this, I realize that everyone who goes through the process of releasing an addiction feels pain. This is true because the pattern that is the addiction is itself the withholding of love, which causes pain. Releasing the addiction is the process of feeling, step by step, a little more love for ourselves. It is this willingness to open steadily to feeling love that weakens and finally dissolves the addiction and the pain.

Since no one who has created an addiction can release it suddenly, the perception of the recovering addict that the process is accompanied by pain is correct. The experience of opening our hearts is the path to releasing pain. The brain controls the physical process, but the heart controls the brain.

If we think of a problem as existing on the ground, the higher we are from the ground, the more aspects of the situation come into our view. This broadens our perspective and increases the choice of solutions. Viewing any situation from the standard of principle is

150

using the broadest perspective possible. This always suggests a resolution. Whether or not we are ready to accept it is our choice.

What, then, is the role of those of us who wish to support people with addictive patterns? First, we must understand that the motivation for change can only come from the person with the addictive pattern. It is impossible for another person to provide that motivation. Next, we feel unconditional love for the person just the way he is, whatever his present behavior may be.

People with addictive patterns give themselves and those they interact with a marvelous opportunity to heighten their awareness of what the human experience is all about. It is about self-love and living in the present. Loving ourselves also means releasing judgment. It is acknowledging that whatever is, is perfect just the way it is.

Individuals with addictive patterns who wish to release them teach themselves and others how to say no with love. They also remind us that life is a feeling experience. It is an opportunity to open our hearts to everyone, embracing all in unconditional love, particularly those who seem most unlovable.

It is only by keeping ourselves separate from someone or something that we introduce fear and pain. Eventually, as we complete the removal of the barriers of separation, we embrace all in love. We realize that nothing is separate from us and Oneness becomes our reality.

# THE ADVANCED COURSE

Many people ask, "Does unconditional love mean that we have to do whatever is requested of us? Does unconditional love mean that we act the same way with all people?"

The answer to the first question is no. Unconditional love is a feeling state. It requires no action. The only action that is appropriate, if action is chosen, is that which is an outgrowth of the feeling of unconditional love.

When a person is in a feeling state of unconditional love, there is no perceived *need to act*. If there is a perceived need to act, it is a signal that the motivation is based on something other than a feeling of unconditional love. Usually it is based on a belief that something is not perfect just the way it is and needs fixing. Then obligation often becomes the motivating factor. The result is discomfort, the signal to choose again. When a person is in doubt, it is preferable not to act but to wait until the choice feels either peaceful and comfortable or inspired by a strong, joyful desire to share a wonderful feeling. An unconditionally loving feeling transforms the perception of linear time. In this state, time ceases to be a factor. Patience replaces urgency, and ease becomes the order of the day.

Does unconditional love mean that we act the same way with all people? The answer again is no.

For those of us who are learning to live our lives based on unconditional love, the transition is a challenging interlude. Being unfamiliar with how to relate to others with an open heart can cause us to misperceive others' intentions. For example, a person feeling

153

what she interprets as unconditional love can perceive a casual male-female interaction as having a deeper meaning.

Unconditional love can be a confusing experience for a novice. Our society has not prepared us to move through life with our hearts open. Care should be taken to become comfortable and conversant with the new feeling state before making any significant decisions based on it. Truth is the best approach. We must be honest with ourselves.

For those who are in a committed relationship, it is preferable to honor it during the transitional period, if possible. Patience and forgiveness are recommended, particularly when one of the two is seeking change and the other prefers to remain as she is.

When one person in a relationship changes, the relationship changes. There comes a time when a new balance point is reached. Waiting until that time arrives gives both people the opportunity to decide, with clarity and in a state of peacefulness, whether or not to continue together.

For many people, the discomfort of changing belief systems can lead to the erroneous conclusion that a change of partners will result in an improvement in how they feel. Remember, no inner change ever occurs as a result of a change outside. Another person cannot cause us to feel joyful or peaceful. A premature change of partners invariably ends up as a change of appearance rather than of substance. Again, it is wise to delay decisions and actions until the motivation for them arises out of inspiration grounded in peacefulness.

It is true that when we are at peace and feeling joyful, the people we meet usually respond in kind. It is also true, however, that at times we find ourselves in circumstances that appear chaotic and are, in fact, uncomfortable for most of the participants. As long as we remain at peace, we do not feel discomfort. *How we feel about a situation determines how we experience it.*

For example, you spend a weekend visiting with your sister and her family. During dinner your sister and her husband have a heated argument. If there is no anger in you, you do not feel their anger. You can still feel their love for each other, which is just being expressed outwardly in a distorted way.

Very often, the presence of a person at peace dominates the energy in a gathering. However, it cannot interfere with a strong intention, such as one to express anger, since free will is always honored in the Universe. When we find that another person's behavior causes us discomfort, it is mirroring a conflict within us. It is an opportunity to release a misperception or replace a withholding of love with forgiveness and love.

The mirror principle is a consistent and accurate gauge to guide us in making changes. If we wish our experiences to be joyful, we must first feel joy within. Since each of us controls how we feel, each of us has the power to experience every event in life in any way we wish.

Everyone and everything reflects peace, love, and joy all the time. We see and feel what we choose. When we see and feel something else, we are seeing our own unclarity and making a judgment based on it.

There is a simple four-step procedure that enables anyone who is willing to release the love that is bound up in judgment. Before you begin to use the procedure, be certain that you are willing to experience it at a feeling level, not an intellectual one. Begin by relaxing and feeling peaceful. Complete each step. Do not proceed with a subsequent step until you feel love at a deep level.

Feel the love of your higher Self.

Feel that same love with the same intensity for yourself.

Feel that same love with the same intensity for the judgment.

Feel that same love with the same intensity for the circumstance or person you are judging.

The process of feeling love for that which we are judging removes the only obstacle to joyfulness. The quality of our lives at any moment reflects precisely how much joy we are willing to allow ourselves to feel. If we wish to allow more, we must prepare ourselves in consciousness. This means heightening our awareness of our inner joyfulness, acknowledging its presence, and consciously choosing to feel it.

We know that we have mastered universal principles when we are able to maintain our inner peace and joyfulness during any and every circumstance. It is the demonstration that we believe that nothing outside of us is ever capable of influencing how we feel. We have aligned completely and consistently with principle, and all of the abundance of the Universe enfolds us.

# EPILOGUE

In most chapters I have drawn a comparison between how our society presently functions and how it can function using universal principles as the standard. This could lead the reader to the conclusion that the latter is better than the former. This is not true. The knowing part of each of us has created life precisely as it is, so that we may experience it just that way.

*Everything each of us does is perfect just the way it is. In fact, it cannot be otherwise, for our Souls have created it. Our only choice is whether or not to see it and feel it as perfect just the way it is.*

As a way to support ourselves in seeing life as perfect just the way it is, the knowing part of us continues to push us up against our resistance to a change in perception. We support each other in this process by mirroring our current perceptions for each other. When we see something in another that really annoys us, angers us, or frightens us, we are really seeing inside ourselves. The very thing that we judge about another reflects the same quality that we are not at peace with in ourselves.

Being at peace with life just the way it is, is achieved through our willingness to forgive each other, at a feeling level, for acting in ways that we previously judged as less than perfect. In forgiving each other, we are really forgiving ourselves. The forgiveness process opens our hearts and, eventually, when the feeling of forgiveness is complete, we accept the fact that no one was ever less than loving toward us.

Whenever we see and feel something other than love around us, we are just seeing a projection of our own misperception. We call it reality, but it is an illusion. This does not mean that whatever

157

we see is a total fantasy. It is just a distortion of reality created by our interpretation of what we are viewing.

All that is required of us is to embrace in love whatever we see just the way it is. It is that simple. It is through our hearts that judgment is released. It is through our hearts that we connect with each other, free of the distortion that our minds create. When we do connect with our hearts, we know that we are invulnerable and that only joy is real.

In the introduction I defined illusion as something we think is real but is not. Now I wish to expand the definition.

The way we create an illusion is through judgment. Judgment is a projection on the outside of the precise ways in which we withhold love from ourselves on the inside. The justifications we have for viewing ourselves as less than lovable form the basis of our perceiving faults in others.

Releasing judgment of others increases our love for ourselves. The expansion of self-love heightens our appreciation for the gifts of the Universe, all of which are presented to us in love. This expansion is the process of distinguishing reality from illusion. It is the deepening of gratitude for the Universe and all its attributes, such as peace, harmony, abundance, and joyfulness.

The next step is the emergence of humility. When we love ourselves enough to feel whole and complete and one with the Universe, we radiate love toward everyone and everything. The feeling within is joyfulness based on gratitude for the beauty of life. It appears to others as humility.

Humility is a quality others see in us. It is acknowledgment by them of our mastery of principle, which in truth is the release of illusion. What is left is reality—the perfection of the Universe, undistorted by the withholding of love from ourselves and others.

I hope this book has given you a greater appreciation for reality and a desire to nurture and support its emergence into our world of illusion.

# APPENDIX

## THE SUPPORT GROUP EXPERIENCE

Many people, after attending my seminars, have chosen to form weekly support groups in their home communities. These support groups allow them to model the way people interact when everyone feels unconditional love so that they can expand this feeling and behavior to the rest of their lives. This Appendix outlines the basis for these support groups and then describes in detail how they operate. The following material is adapted from my first book, *You Can Have It All.*

The Universe functions as a mutual support system. Everything in the Universe relates to everything else. The sun provides the energy for growth of plants, which in turn provide food for animals. The planets exert gravitational influences on each other. Our use of the resources on our planet influences the quality of the air we breathe and the water we drink. Since every thought has some impact on the physical universe, each of us is continually influencing the quality of our environment. We are part of a mutual support system.

Our ability to function successfully within a mutual support system is related to our willingness to recognize and believe that this is indeed the nature of our life experience. Society tends to teach us differently. It encourages us to strike our on our own and work to achieve personal objectives and goals. We are left with the impression that we can achieve happiness at the expense of others, or at least without caring about others.

It is important, then, to keep reminding ourselves that the Universe creates us to function in the context of a mutual support system. The more mindful we are of the interrelatedness of each and every person and thing in the Universe, the more we enjoy the benefit of the perfect design of the universal system.

The basic laws of the Universe are the guidelines for life within this mutual support system. Following them places us in alignment with everyone and everything within the system.

We see this mutual support system functioning, to varying degrees, within families, clubs, associations, religious organizations, and businesses.

When we operate within the world of illusion, we often establish rules and standards for groups that are not in alignment with the basic laws of the Universe. Therefore, as you may have noticed, many groups do not provide a comfortable level of support for their members.

It is possible for people everywhere to create support groups for themselves. These five simple guidelines will enable a group of people (a group is two or more people) to act as a mutual support group.

## SEE THE PERFECTION IN EVERYTHING

This is a reminder that we experience everything the way we perceive it. There is no event that is good or bad, right or wrong. Consider once again the example of the cut finger. You can become angry at yourself for causing yourself pain. Or you can be thankful that the Universe, through the pain, is reminding you of a self-destructive tendency that you can release and replace with behavior that is self-supportive and pleasurable, now that it is brought to your attention.

## STATE EVERYTHING IN PRESENT TIME

The only time that ever exists is the present moment. (The past is gone forever and the future is yet to be.) Each of us can be so completely in the present moment that we are at one with it. As we learn to trust the Universe more, we allow ourselves to focus more in the present moment and to be

160

more at peace with it. By stating our thoughts in the present tense, we are continually reminding ourselves of this principle.

## EVERYONE SUPPORTS EVERYONE ELSE

This is a reminder that we are part of a mutual support system. We are all dependent upon one another. As we support each other, we support ourselves.

## BEING AT PEACE WITH WHAT IS

We improve the quality of our life by first accepting that our life is the way it is because we are being guided by our knowingness (Soul).

Our choice is to either see the perfection in this process or to resist seeing it. As soon as we see and feel the perfection of our life just the way it is, and are at peace with it, we are led to our next lesson. As long as we resist, the same lesson is repeated.

Learning to make peace with what is opens us to the joyfulness within. The more we focus on this joyfulness and feel it, the more it fills our life. We can allow it to expand so that it fills us with its warmth and happiness. This is our real self. As we cultivate it and nurture it, it will grow to fill our life with its presence.

When we express joy, we draw it out of those we meet, creating joyful people and joyful events. The greater the joy we express, the more joy we experience, until, eventually, we realize that only joy is real.

## EVERYONE GENTLY, KINDLY, AND LOVINGLY
## REMINDS EVERYONE ELSE OF THE GUIDELINES
## WHEN THEY ARE NOT BEING OBSERVED

It is the responsibility of each member of the group to keep the group on purpose. This is done in a gentle, kind, and loving manner. Any story can be told, any event recounted, or any problem presented in a way that is in alignment with the principles discussed in this book. It helps everyone to guide the presenter toward an approach that supports him and the others in the group.

The foregoing guidelines served to launch the support system. However, additional guidelines were needed to maintain the focus of the group whenever a participant presented a personal problem.

THE ELEVEN STEPS is just such a guideline. It contains a series of suggestions and questions that enables the presenter to perceive the problem in the context of universal principles.

To increase the effectiveness of the procedure, the other participants remain silent while the presenter speaks. It is an active silence, however, with each person focusing attention and support on the presenter. The major function of the listener is to provide so much love and support for the presenter that he feels free to say what is true for him at that moment. The insights gained by the presenter during this experience prove invaluable in assisting with the resolution of the problem.

## THE ELEVEN STEPS
## (PROCEDURE TO REPERCEIVE A PROBLEM)

When a participant presents to the group a situation that is causing him discomfort, the following step-by-step procedure is suggested. A member of the group reads the following instructions, one at a time, allowing the person with the situation to respond to each instruction before proceeding to the next one.

### DEFINE THE SITUATION

This step is to allow the person to explain, as briefly as possible, what is causing the discomfort. Once the situation has been defined, the exercise can begin.

CLOSE YOUR EYES AND BECOME AWARE OF THE
FEELING IN YOUR BODY, SEPARATE FROM ANY
THOUGHTS YOU MAY HAVE ABOUT IT. INDICATE
WHEN THE DISCOMFORT LEAVES.

The reason for this step is to help the person separate the
feelings in his body from all thoughts he may have about
them. The chapter on emotion explains the importance of
this. As long as a thought is attached to a feeling, discomfort is experienced in our bodies.

ARE YOU WILLING TO TAKE TOTAL RESPONSIBILITY
FOR ALL ASPECTS OF THE SITUATION? IN WHAT
WAY?

This question is a reminder that we determine how we experience our life.

DO YOU AGREE THAT NOTHING YOU OR ANYONE
ELSE HAS DONE OR IS DOING IS EITHER WRONG
OR RIGHT?    PLEASE EXPLAIN.

This question reminds the presenter that as long as he is
judging himself or anyone else, he stays locked in the discomfort he is presently experiencing. The only way to release the discomfort is to release all judgment of everyone
and everything, including himself.

DO YOU REALIZE THAT YOU ARE RECEIVING
EXACTLY WHAT YOU WANT AND THE OTHER
PERSON IS RECEIVING EXACTLY WHAT HE WANTS?
PLEASE EXPLAIN.

This is a reminder that our Soul creates the events of our life
as a way of guiding us to release our misperceptions
through forgiveness and opening our hearts.

DO YOU RECOGNIZE THAT THE WAY YOU SEE THE
OTHER PERSON IS REALLY THE WAY YOU SEE
YOURSELF? DO YOU WISH TO SHARE AN EXAMPLE?

This is a restatement of the mirror principle.

**DO YOU REALIZE THAT WHAT YOU ARE EXPERIENCING IS PRECISELY HOW YOU SEE THE SITUATION?**

This is a reminder that the way you see others or situations is a reflection of your state of consciousness. It is the most efficient way to find out what you really believe.

**PERCEIVE THE SITUATION DIFFERENTLY. CREATE ANOTHER INTERPRETATION OF IT.**

Everything we experience is a result of our perception of it. When our perception changes, the experience changes. In order for a person to perceive a troubling situation in a different way, he must let go of his attachment to his present perception of the situation. It is his unwillingness to do this that is a major cause of the situation in the first place. After a couple of minutes of meditation, if the presenter is unable to perceive the situation differently, he is told to continue meditating on this step at home until he is successful in perceiving it differently.

My experience has taught me that while suggestions from others in the group as to how the presenter can perceive the situation differently may appear to benefit the presenter, in the long run only the presenter's self-initiated change in perception of the situation is of lasting benefit.

**PLEASE DESCRIBE THE WAYS YOU ARE WITHHOLDING LOVE FROM YOURSELF AND OTHERS.**

All discomfort involves a witholding of love. Locating the witholding helps to clarify what is really going on.

**GO BEHIND THE APPARENT CIRCUMSTANCES OF THE SITUATION AND LOCATE THE LOVE IN**

YOURSELF AND IN ALL OTHERS INVOLVED IN THE
SITUATION.

This is a reminder that the only true motivation for all behavior is love. When anyone's behavior is less than loving, it is just the closest that the person can come at that moment to expressing love.

FEEL THE JOY THAT COMES WHEN THE LOVE IS
FOUND AND EXPRESSED.

This puts a person in touch with what is always there, if he looks for it.

The foregoing guidelines are designed to keep the participants of a support group in alignment with the basic principles of the Universe. A support group can function as a perfect family, giving each participant the opportunity to practice the principles in a safe, supportive environment. As each participant learns that life outside the support group is not different from life inside, he experiments with the use of the principles in all settings of his life. Many participants in existing support groups have successfully transferred their mastery of the principles to their lives outside the support groups, thereby allowing their whole world to be a support system. Remember, *we experience life the way we perceive it.*

When using THE ELEVEN STEPS, one of the participants in the group acts as the leader and guides the person with the situation through the procedure. The group listens attentively, *making no response.* This way the presenter learns what he really believes about the issues raised by each step in the process.

Learning the truth about our beliefs is the first step in changing them. Once we know what they are, we can begin to take responsibility for them. Once we truly understand that we have created our beliefs in the first place, we know that only we have the power to change them.

───────

## SUGGESTED OUTLINE FOR A TYPICAL SUPPORT GROUP MEETING

START ON TIME.

SELECT A LEADER FOR THE MEETING.

Alternate leaders at subsequent meetings. Choose, as leader, a person who is feeling happy and is eager to support others.

CENTER THE ENERGY IN THE GROUP.

Sit in a circle and have the leader focus everyone's attention on a thought such as, "We are all grateful for the opportunity to be together and to offer our love and support to each other."

THE ELEVEN STEPS.

Each person announces a number between one and ten. A high number indicates that it is important to the person that he have the opportunity to go through THE ELEVEN STEPS at the meeting. More than one person can announce the same number.

The leader takes each participant (high numbers first) who wishes to do so, through THE ELEVEN STEPS.

The participant (now the presenter) is free to stop the exercise at any time. It is always his choice, as the group is there to support the presenter.

It is important to remember that no participant is to suggest a solution to a presenter, either during or after the exercise. THE ELEVEN STEPS is the sole method used to deal with the situation being presented. Solutions suggested by others are not helpful. Meaningful changes occur for the presenter only when he gains his own insight as to the solution of his situation.

Feeling the unconditional love and support of the group

provides the presenter with the environment of safety that encourages him to tell the truth to himself. Each member allows whatever the presenter says to be perfect, whether or not he agrees with the statement. This enables the group to feel what unconditional love and support is like.

If the presenter has any difficulty with step 8 (PERCEIVE THE SITUATION DIFFERENTLY) of THE ELEVEN STEPS, the leader suggests that the presenter continue with step 8 at home. The exercise is then continued by proceeding to the next step.

## EACH PARTICIPANT READS HIS INDIVIDUAL PURPOSE

The group members feel the statement with the presenter as it is read.

## READ THE GROUP PURPOSE

To arrive at the group purpose, each member, on his own, defines his purpose for the group. Each member then reads his statement of purpose for the group, which then arrives at a single statement of group purpose.

It is important that the statement reflect the group's purpose on a feeling level. The participants hold hands as they read the statement aloud together. Modifications are suggested until every member feels inspired when the statement is read.

The group purpose is read and felt by the entire group at every meeting. Whenever the purpose ceases to feel inspiring, it is time to modify it.

## THE FEELING EXERCISE

Each person, in turn, closes her eyes and scans her body, noticing how she feels. Feeling fine, she enjoys and expands this wonderful feeling. However, if any feeling of discomfort is noticed, she relaxes into it until it is released. The person then expands the feeling of relaxation into a feeling of joyfulness, peacefulness, or any other feeling chosen, remaining there for a few moments. When the exercise has been completed, she opens her eyes and the next person begins. After all participants have finished, they hold hands and feel their chosen feelings together.

REVIEW A PRINCIPLE.

Select a principle and read it together. It can be the focus of all members until the next meeting.

REQUESTS FOR SPECIFIC SUPPORT.

Each person makes a request for specific support. Remember that all improvement in the quality of one's life begins in consciousness. The request for support focuses on support in consciousness. For example, a person is having difficulty in forgiving a friend. The request to the group is for support in feeling forgiveness for the friend and for herself. Once a person is able to make a clear request for support in consciousness, success is guaranteed. The only variable is the willingness of the person requesting the support to sustain the clear intention to achieve the desired result. Asking for the support strengthens the commitment to oneself.

Another example is of a person experiencing a shortage of cash flow. That person may request support for repeating the definition of abundance in front of the mirror until he feels the abundance of the Universe at a deep feeling level; and for continually acknowledging all of the abundance he presently has.

After the request for specific support is stated, the group responds to the member, "_____, we unconditionally love and support you just the way you are in all your magnificence."

EACH PERSON STATES WAYS IN WHICH USE OF THE PRINCIPLES HAS BEEN HELPFUL OR BENEFICIAL

AND WAYS IN WHICH REQUESTS FOR SUPPORT
HAVE BEEN HELPFUL.

## THE POSITIVE REFLECTION EXERCISE.

In this exercise, group members see positive qualities in each of the other members of the group, which are reflected in themselves.

For example: In looking at one person you realize she has qualities of gentleness and kindness. In looking at another person you immediately feel his humor and joyfulness.

The exercise is carried out in this manner:

> Each participant receives a description of his positive qualities from every member of the group in turn. Then the next person in the group becomes the recipient.

> The person speaking looks directly into the eyes of the recipient and says, "Positive qualities I see in you, that you reflect to me are: _____."

> The recipient responds by saying, "Thank you."

> The exercise continues until every group member has had a chance to be a recipient.

This exercise demonstrates the principle behind giving and receiving. When a person gives acknowledgment to another, he is really acknowledging himself. It is a simultaneous gift from the giver to himself. This is a very powerful exercise. As the group bonds and the members deepen their appreciation for each other, the exercise serves to anchor and expand the depth of their feelings.

This exercise may be done periodically or upon request.

ENGAGE IN A FUN ACTIVITY SUCH AS GROUP
SINGING OR A GROUP GAME.

SET THE DATE AND TIME FOR THE NEXT MEETING.

END THE MEETING ON TIME.

Note: For information on how to connect with the network of support groups, contact:

Katharine Deleot
P.O. Box 450354
Atlanta, GA 30345

Bea Barabas
P.O. Box 4825
San Diego, CA 92104

# GLOSSARY

**ABUNDANCE**   The natural state of affairs in the Universe. If anyone experiences less than total abundance in each and every aspect of life, he or she is resisting the abundance or pushing it away.

**COMMITMENT**   Reaching a 100 percent intention to achieve a result.

**CREATION**   There is "Creation" and "creation." The Universe is Creating all of the time. When we align with It as co-Creators, we Create also. When we create with our conscious minds, as separate from the rest of the Universe, we create only illusions. We know which we are doing by how it feels. When we feel peaceful and unconditionally loving, we are co-Creating. Since love is the sole motivating force in the Universe, true Creation can only occur when love is felt. Creation never ends, as the Universe is always in a state of expansion.

**EMOTION**   An attachment of a thought to a feeling. Thoughts wish to flow freely through our minds and feelings wish to flow freely through our bodies. Attaching a thought to a feeling creates an energy block that we feel as discomfort. Love can be felt; it cannot be described. The attempt to describe or define it moves our focus from our hearts to our heads and blocks the feeling.

**FEAR**   A witholding of love from ourselves, and often from another. It is reversible by feeling love for ourselves or another. The difficulty we have in achieving the reversal is just an indication of the amount of resistance we have to loving ourselves.

**FORGIVENESS**   Reminding ourselves that our judgment of another is really a judgment of ourselves. We feel forgiveness to re-

171

lease the pain that holding on to judgment creates. Forgiveness frees the love in us as we cease withholding it from each other.

**GIVING AND RECEIVING**  The way we experience abundance. Since love is the sole motivating force in the Universe, we are either giving and receiving love or withholding it. When we give it to another, we are really giving it to ourselves. Giving love creates joy for the giver. This is the most valuable gift we can give ourselves.

**JUDGMENT**  See NONJUDGMENT.

**LOVE**  The sole motivating force in the Universe. All energy is a form of love. If an experience creates less than joyfulness, it means love is being withheld in some way.

**MEANS AND ENDS**  These are identical. The means chosen to achieve a particular result is the result. If we wish to experience inner peace, we must live each day in a peaceful manner.

**MIRROR PRINCIPLE**  Whatever we experience is a reflection of the state of our consciousness at that moment. It is the brilliant way the Universe supports us in seeing what is inside us, what we really believe. We support each other in the learning experience by mirroring for each other. If a person acts in a way that causes us to feel angry, he is just reflecting our own anger. He or his behavior is not the cause of the anger. He is just the catalyst who helps us demonstrate our own anger to us.

**NONJUDGMENT**  Right and wrong, good and bad are perceptual distortions that block the flow of love within and from the person making the judgment. Every event is just an occurrence to be experienced and accepted just the way it is. When we judge anyone or anything, we are really judging ourselves.

**PAIN**  The way we experience fear in our physical bodies.

**PERFECTION**  The Universe is always functioning perfectly. We can either choose to see and feel the perfection or insist that our interpretation of the situation as imperfect is accurate. Since love is the sole motivating force in the Universe, we can always see and feel love, if we are willing. This often means seeing beyond the way a person is acting and resonating with her Essence, which is love.

## PURPOSE

**Individual Purpose**  Defining for ourselves our relationship to the Universe. It is the awareness of our role in the larger scheme of things. It is feeling our connection to the Universe and aligning ourselves with our understanding of the purpose of the Universe. Our purpose must be bigger than we are. It serves to give our lives focus and meaning. It inspires us to feel love for the Universe, ourselves, and others. This inspiration prepares the way for us. We feel our copartnership with the Universe and Its support in leading us through our lives.

*Example:* My purpose is seeing the perfection in everyone and everything, and feeling love for myself and others just the way we are.

**Group Purpose**  Defining the way two or more people align themselves with each other and with the Universe as they pursue any venture together.

*Example:* Our purpose in forming our support group is to expand our unconditional love and support for each other, deepen our sense of Oneness, and feel the joy of sharing our real selves.

**Purpose for a Specific Undertaking**  Our individual purpose establishes our awareness of the context of our lives in the broadest sense. Before we embark on a particular venture or activity that is more than casual, it is most helpful to define our purpose for pursuing it. Although the focus of the venture is specific, the purpose, the true motivation for it, can be broad and universal. Defining our purpose for the venture in universal terms aligns all of the elements involved in the venture with our individual purpose. This

173

broad perspective not only inspires us to proceed, it also sets up the feeling of copartnership with the Universe and invites the path-clearing it provides.

*Example:* My purpose in applying for a position as an executive of a company is to have fun, feel joyful, and share my administrative talents in a creative and loving manner with all those who interact with me.

**SUPPORT**   The Universe is a mutual support system. Everything is designed to support everything else. When we see it differently, our perception is amiss. Every situation we experience as nonsupportive can become supportive when we change our perception of it.

**TRANSITIONAL PERIOD**   The time when old beliefs are not yet released and trust in universal principles is not complete. It is a time of uncertainty, since either the old or the new beliefs can be operative at any given time.

**IN UNIVERSAL TERMS**   Defining a situation or seeing it in accordance with universal principles. This requires a willingness to release, at least temporarily, preconceived ideas and prior experiences as a basis for decisions.

**THE UNIVERSE HANDLES THE DETAILS**   This is the way the Universe encourages us to align with It and use universal principles as the guidelines for our lives. It only handles those details that support us in following the principles. When we choose other standards or guidelines, we must ourselves handle all the details that arise in connection with that choice.

Mr. Patent's books are available at many bookstores, or you may order them directly from:

Celebration Publishing
P.O. Box 336
Piermont, New York 10968
(914) 353-1677